HOW TO WIN IN SPORTS FOR YOUNG ATHLETES

A GUIDE FOR YOUNG ATHLETES, PARENTS, COACHES
AND ANYONE WHO WANTS TO WIN IN LIFE

JACK WALIA

CONTENTS

INTRODUCTION

Eight-year-old Mia positioned herself at the starting line for her very first track meet. She felt her heart racing and her hands becoming moist. She observed the other kids, who seemed prepared and self-assured. Doubt slowly started to take hold. Is it possible for her to do this? With a deep breath, she recalled her coach's words: "Today's outcome isn't about winning or losing."

This book, "How to Win in Sports for Young People," aims to provide young athletes, parents, and coaches with proven and practical mental techniques to excel in sports and life. Mental resilience is not limited to elite athletes alone.

Mental toughness is vital to achieve success. It's about resilience, perseverance, and having a positive mindset. These attributes assist young athletes in recovering from obstacles, remaining composed during challenging situations, and persevering through tough times. Building mental resilience from a young age lays the groundwork for future success in all areas.

The book was created with a wide range of readers in mind by the author. It is designed for young athletes looking to enhance their performance, parents wanting to support their children's sports goals, coaches aiming to bring out their teams' best, and regular individuals seeking to maximize their potential in life. Regardless of your experience level, this book has something to offer you.

The book is organized into multiple chapters, with each one centered on mental toughness. We'll cover goal setting, managing pressure, overcoming failure, and boosting confidence. Real-life examples and case studies of successful athletes are featured in every chapter.

One example is the story of Michael Jordan, who was rejected from his high school basketball team but went on to become one of the greatest players in history. You will also discover how regular people have achieved greatness through mental strength in different areas.

This book guarantees effective techniques that you can apply. These techniques are easy to comprehend and put into practice, making them accessible to all. Discover tips for staying motivated, strategies for maintaining focus, and exercises to build resilience.

Our focus will be on tackling typical obstacles and objections. How do you handle moments when you want to quit? What is your approach to dealing with criticism and setbacks? The book provides answers to these questions and suggests ways to overcome these obstacles.

I wrote this book because I'm passionate about helping young athletes, parents, coaches, and everyday people overcome mental obstacles. I have witnessed the life-changing power of mental toughness myself. Anyone can achieve unmatched success in sports and life with the right mindset and tools.

Stay open-minded and be ready to experiment with new techniques as you read this book. Certain techniques may be more effective for you than others. Discovering what works best for you and practicing diligently is crucial. Developing mental toughness is a skill that requires time, but the rewards are worth it.

I want to share a quote that has always inspired me:

> *"Success is not final, failure is not fatal: It is the courage to continue that counts."*
>
> — WINSTON CHURCHILL

Let's start this journey together. Discover the mental strategies for winning in sports and life. The journey is about to begin.

1

MENTAL TOUGHNESS

Sarah was nervous when she first entered the basketball court. According to her coach, it's not only about skill. That's the distinction between being good and being great. Sarah understood that her mindset would be the ultimate factor in determining her success, even though physical training was important. Her focus shifted towards developing mental toughness, resulting in a transformative impact on her game and life. This chapter is designed to enhance your comprehension of mental toughness and its significance in sports and beyond.

THE SIGNIFICANCE OF MENTAL TOUGHNESS: DEFINITION AND IMPORTANCE.

Mental toughness means remaining focused, confident, and resilient in high-pressure situations. It provides motivation during difficult times, enabling peak performance in even the toughest situations. Picture yourself in a high-stakes game. We're under tremendous pressure, and the whole world is watching. With mental toughness, you can remain calm, composed, and focused, making the right moves and decisions even under stress.

Reflect on the remarkable "Flu Game" played by Michael Jordan on June 11, 1997. Despite being severely affected by food poisoning, he managed to score 38 points, leading the Chicago Bulls to win. His mental strength is evident in his exceptional performance despite challenging circumstances. Despite physical discomfort, he remained focused. Serena Williams has demonstrated remarkable resilience of the mind as well. Her ability to come from behind and win in many matches is an inspiration to athletes worldwide, showcasing resilience and determination. By leading his team to victory against all odds, Tom Brady's Super Bowl performances showcase the power of mental strength.

Enhancing mental resilience can boost your performance. Maintaining calmness and focus during high-pressure situations leads to improved performance. Additionally, it aids in alleviating anxiety. Rather than feeling overwhelmed by stress, you develop skills to effectively manage it. Your overall performance is improved by your ability to handle stress and setbacks. It results in improved outcomes across different areas of life. Added advantages include increased confidence and self-belief. Confidence flourishes when you know you can handle pressure, increasing belief in your abilities. Self-belief can be a game-changer, impacting all aspects of your life.

Mental toughness consists of key components like focus, resilience, and emotional control. Staying concentrated on the task at hand is what focus is about. Whether it's during practice or a competition, staying focused is crucial for giving your best effort. Bouncing back from setbacks is what defines resilience. Every person encounters obstacles and disappointments, but resilient individuals refuse to be defined by them. They learn from their mistakes and keep moving forward.

Managing your emotions is the essence of emotional regulation. It's normal to feel nervous or stressed, but managing these emotions prevents them from affecting your performance.

Begin developing mental resilience by establishing specific and attainable objectives. Divide your long-term objectives into smaller, achievable tasks. Staying focused and motivated is simplified by this approach. Mindfulness practice can be beneficial as well. Engaging in breathing exercises or meditation can enhance your ability to remain present and concentrated. Another effective tool is positive self-talk. Swap out negative thoughts for positive affirmations. Replace the thought of "I can't do this" with "I am capable and resilient."

Don't forget, it takes time to develop the skill of mental toughness. Dealing with pressure and stress is not about never feeling them, but about how you handle these challenges. With these techniques, you can develop mental resilience and succeed in both sports and life. Mental toughness applies to more than just elite athletes. It's a skill that can greatly enhance performance and goal attainment. Mental toughness can greatly impact anyone's path to success, whether you're an athlete, parent, coach, or just an ordinary person.

THE GROWTH MINDSET: HOW TO EMBRACE LEARNING AND IMPROVEMENT

Picture Alex, a young soccer player, experiencing frustration when he misses a goal or makes a mistake in practice. He thinks his abilities are fixed and his efforts won't lead to progress. It's a classic case of having a fixed mindset. In the fixed mindset, abilities and talents are seen as unchangeable and static. Individuals who possess a fixed mindset tend to shy away from challenges due to their fear of failure and criticism. Instead of seeing mistakes as chances to learn and grow, they view them as a reflection of their inherent limitations.

On the other hand, a growth mindset believes that individuals can improve their abilities through effort and learning. Psychologist Carol Dweck popularized this mindset, which shows that those with a growth mindset embrace challenges, persist through difficulties, and see failure as a path to success. Young athletes must adopt a growth mindset to build mental resilience. It helps build resilience by motivating them to persevere through obstacles. Alex's view on soccer shifted as he grasped the idea of a growth mindset. Rather than dwelling on his mistakes, he viewed each missed goal as a chance to learn and improve.

Adopting a growth mindset has extensive benefits. It brings about enhanced resilience when dealing with obstacles. Athletes who have faith in their ability to improve are more likely to persevere during challenging periods. Mental toughness requires persistence and determination. The ability to learn from mistakes is also improved by a growth mindset. Athletes with a growth mindset don't let failure defeat them; instead, they analyze their mistakes and use that knowledge to improve, driving overall success.

What are the ways to cultivate a growth mindset? Start by emphasizing effort over innate talent.

Acknowledge the effort and commitment put into growth rather than focusing solely on the outcome. Understand that consistent effort and practice lead to improvement. Embrace the opportunity to learn from failures. Consider the lessons you can gather from mistakes. Valuable lessons arise from setbacks through this reflection. Instead of solely focusing on winning, set goals that prioritize improvement and learning. The goals need to be specific, measurable, and attainable, offering a clear route for development.

Take a look at an actual case study. Let's think about Steph Curry's story. Despite being ignored by top colleges and facing doubts about his size, Curry dedicated himself to constant practice and learning from every game. Early obstacles didn't shape his identity. Rather, he utilized them as a driving force to increase his efforts. Today, he is known as one of the best shooters in NBA history, proving the strength of a growth mindset.

Academics also provide another example. A student with math difficulties embraced the concept of growth mindset. Rather than quitting, she actively sought additional assistance, maintained a consistent practice routine, and embraced every mistake as an opportunity to learn. Her grades saw a significant improvement over time, and she gained newfound confidence in her abilities. Her academic performance and overall approach to life's challenges improved due to this shift in mindset.

To foster a growth mindset in young athletes, parents and coaches can promote an environment that values effort and learning. Give feedback that highlights areas for improvement rather than solely pointing out errors. Recognize any progress, even the smallest, to reinforce the belief that hard work and perseverance lead to improvement. Cultivate a culture that embraces challenges and recognizes mistakes as opportunities for growth.

Utilizing these methods can have a major impact. It encourages young athletes to face challenges, overcome obstacles, and seek growth. The growth mindset is a powerful tool that builds mental toughness, resilience, and a love for learning in all aspects of life, not just sports.

GRIT AND PERSEVERANCE: THE SCIENCE BEHIND NEVER GIVING UP

Success often hinges on the unappreciated qualities of grit and perseverance. Grit involves the desire and persistence to achieve long-term objectives. The motivation to achieve your dreams remains even when the initial excitement fades. Perseverance entails persisting despite challenges or setbacks. It provides motivation during tough times and distant goals. Long-term success is heavily reliant on perseverance and initial excitement.

Much of Angela Duckworth's research has focused on understanding grit. According to her, it involves blending passion and perseverance. According to her research, grit is a stronger predictor of success than talent or intelligence. Duckworth explains in her book "Grit: The Power of Passion and Perseverance" how remarkable achievements can be attained through grit. High levels of grit increase the likelihood of success in different areas, including education, sports, and business. Cultivating grit in young athletes is underscored by this correlation.

To develop grit, one must establish long-term objectives and divide them into smaller, achievable tasks. This method reduces the overwhelm and increases the attainability of ambitious goals. To become a champion swimmer, begin by setting smaller goals like improving lap time or mastering new strokes. This approach maintains your motivation and offers a straightforward direction to pursue. It's important to also prioritize consistent practice and effort. Building discipline and resilience is possible by establishing a routine with regular practice. Evaluating past achievements and setbacks can boost your perseverance. By examining successes and failures, you can gain valuable insights and cultivate resilience.

Take into account the inspiring journey of Wilma Rudolph, who triumphed over major challenges to reach her aspirations. She endured polio as a child and was warned she may never regain the ability to walk. Nevertheless, she persisted. With relentless effort and dedication, she mastered the art of walking. In the 1960 Olympics, she secured three gold medals and became the fastest woman on earth. The impact of grit and perseverance is powerfully demonstrated in her story.

J. K. Rowling is another example that is inspiring. Before the success of Harry Potter, she faced many rejections from publishers and struggled with financial difficulties. She persisted in writing and refining her manuscript, despite these obstacles. She never gave up and is now one of the world's most successful authors. Rowling's story demonstrates how persistence can result in remarkable achievements, despite facing multiple failures.

These practical tips will assist you in cultivating grit.

1. Break down your long-term goals into smaller, actionable steps for better clarity. This will help you stay focused and make the process less intimidating.
2. Create a schedule that involves regular practice and hard work. Consistency plays a crucial role in developing grit, whether it's consistent training or regular study sessions.
3. Take a moment to think about your past experiences.

Honor your achievements and derive lessons from your setbacks. This self-reflection aids in identifying strengths and areas for growth, fostering resilience in the process.

You can make a big impact by implementing these strategies into your life. Whether you're a high-achieving athlete or an individual chasing personal aspirations, grit and perseverance are vital for success. By developing these characteristics, you can conquer challenges, fulfill aspirations, and motivate others.

DEVELOPING EMOTIONAL INTELLIGENCE: MANAGING EMOTIONS FOR BETTER PERFORMANCE

EI, short for emotional intelligence, significantly impacts an athlete's performance and well-being. Emotional intelligence involves recognizing, understanding, and managing our own emotions and the emotions of others. The five major components include self-awareness, self-regulation, motivation, empathy, and social skills. Being self-aware means acknowledging and understanding how your emotions affect you. It's like taking a step back and observing the connection between your emotions and actions. For instance, recognizing that pre-game nervousness is normal and addressing it instead of letting it escalate into anxiety.

Self-regulation involves managing emotions and impulses. The skill of maintaining calmness and composure, even in high-stress situations. Athletes must not allow frustration from mistakes or bad calls to impact their overall performance. LeBron James is a prime example of self-regulation, staying composed under pressure and making calculated decisions that benefit his team. In the context of EI, motivation stems from internal reasons rather than external rewards, driving individuals to achieve their goals. It's about having a passion for what you do and a drive to get better. Athletes who are highly motivated, practice skills fueled by an internal drive for excellence, not just the desire to win.

Empathy requires comprehending and empathizing with others' emotions. Cooperation and mutual support are vital in team sports, making it a critical component. A coach who understands their players' struggles can provide more practical guidance and support. Social skills involve effectively influencing others towards desired outcomes. Athletes need to work together, cooperate, and communicate effectively with teammates and coaches. Developing strong social skills contributes to creating a united and supportive team atmosphere.

Emotional intelligence is valuable in more than just sports. Athletes who possess high emotional intelligence perform better by effectively handling their emotions, remaining focused, and maintaining composure in high-pressure situations. This emotional regulation enhances performance. EI fosters strong relationships with teammates, coaches, and others, leading to a positive and supportive atmosphere for greater success. Emotional intelligence extends beyond the field and enhances overall well-being and life satisfaction. By effectively understanding and managing emotions, individuals can better navigate life's challenges, leading to a more balanced and fulfilling existence.

Cultivating emotional intelligence demands ongoing dedication and practice. Self-awareness and self-regulation can be improved through mindfulness and self-reflection. Devoting a few minutes daily to contemplate on your emotions and their influence can enhance self-awareness. Developing empathy can be achieved through active listening. When you listen to others, focus on understanding their perspective without offering solutions or judgments.

Strengthening relationships and building a supportive network can be achieved through this practice. Employing relaxation techniques like deep breathing, meditation, or progressive muscle relaxation can assist in maintaining composure and managing stress. Self-motivation can be developed through setting and achieving personal goals. When you prioritize goals that match your values and passions, you can harness an internal motivation that pushes you forward.

Consider this real-life situation. Think about a sports player who faced challenges with performance anxiety. Through mindfulness and relaxation techniques, they improved their emotional regulation and remained calm and focused during competitions. This improvement in emotional intelligence led to better performance and increased confidence.

A coach who utilized empathy and social skills achieved success with their team. By understanding the needs of their players and promoting open communication, they created a supportive and positive environment. By adopting this approach, team dynamics were enhanced and resulted in remarkable success in the field.

Adding emotional intelligence to your daily routine can have a big impact. Whether you're an athlete or someone pursuing personal growth, developing emotional intelligence can improve how you handle emotions, form strong connections, and reach your goals.

THE POWER OF POSITIVE SELF-TALK: REWIRING YOUR INNER DIALOGUE

Positive self-talk encourages confidence, motivation, and a positive perspective through internal dialogue. The inner voice encourages you, saying "I can do this" and "I have what it takes." Damaging effects can result from negative self-talk. It's that relentless inner voice that constantly undermines, whispering "I can't," "I'm inadequate," or "I'll never achieve." For example, if a young athlete believes they won't make the team, they may not try hard enough to succeed, thus validating their negative thinking.For example, if a young athlete believes they won't make the team, they may not try hard enough to succeed, thus validating their negative thinking.

The effects of negative self-talk are significant. It can result in reduced motivation, impaired performance, and heightened anxiety. Doubting your abilities leads to hesitation and reduces your willingness to take risks, which limits your growth and development. Your physical performance can be influenced by negative self-talk as well. When a gymnast doubts their ability to execute a routine, they may tense up and make errors, but positive self-talk can maintain relaxation and concentration.

Engaging in positive self-talk helps combat negative thoughts and cultivate mental resilience. Begin by recognizing and questioning negative thoughts. Before you continue thinking, take a moment to question the accuracy and helpfulness of your thoughts. When you think, "I'm going to fail," counter that thought by questioning, "What proof do I have of my failure?Substitute it with a positive affirmation such as "I am confident, capable and destined for success."

Positive affirmations can be useful when created and practiced. Compile a collection of positive affirmations that resonate with you and recite them daily. Make sure your affirmations are specific, positive, and centered around your abilities and potential. Examples include phrases like "I possess resilience" or "I am equipped with the necessary skills and determination to achieve success."

Positive self-talk can be strengthened through visualization techniques. Picture yourself achieving all your goals with your eyes closed. Imagine yourself excelling, radiating confidence, and attaining success. Making use of all your senses during visualization can enhance its potency. Take, for instance, if you're a swimmer, imagine yourself diving into the pool, feeling the water, and swimming with power and accuracy. Your confidence can be enhanced and your readiness for real performance can be improved through this mental rehearsal.

Reflect on the experience of a young tennis player who battled with self-doubt. Whenever she entered the court, she was haunted by thoughts of failure. The coach told her to replace negative thoughts with empowering affirmations like "I am strong" and "I am prepared from hard training" to practice positive self-talk.

Another instance involves a public speaker who has a fear of speaking to large audiences. He began substituting negative self-talk with positive affirmations such as "I am a confident and captivating speaker" and "I possess valuable perspectives to contribute."

The power of positive self-talk can enhance mental toughness and performance. By substituting negative thoughts with positive affirmations and visualizing success, you can develop the confidence and concentration required to thrive in sports and life.

SETTING SMART GOALS: A ROADMAP TO ACHIEVING SUCCESS

Setting the right goals is the key to success in sports and life. SMART goals are an effective method for goal setting. The acronym SMART represents Specific, Measurable,

Achievable, Relevant, and Time-bound. These standards assist in establishing objectives that are both clear and achievable, enabling you to stay motivated and focused.

The clarity of specific goals eliminates any ambiguity. Rather than setting a broad goal like "I want to be better at soccer," it is better to have a specific goal like "I want to enhance my dribbling skills."

To track your progress, measurable goals have defined criteria. Let's say you want to enhance your dribbling skills. If that's the case, you can track your progress by aiming to successfully complete a dribbling drill ten times consecutively. Having measurable goals allows you to track your progress and remain motivated.

Goals that are achievable are both realistic and attainable. The tasks should challenge you, but remain achievable. When you set a goal that cannot be achieved, it can result in frustration and loss of motivation. Setting a goal to run a marathon in a month is unrealistic for beginners. Rather, focus on gradually increasing your endurance and aim to complete a 5k in a few months.

Your values and long-term objectives are aligned with relevant goals. They need to be important and help you achieve your ultimate goals. To become a pro soccer player, it's important to enhance your dribbling skills. Remaining committed and focused is ensured by this relevance.

Setting goals with deadlines adds urgency and helps prioritize your efforts. To illustrate, if your goal is to enhance your dribbling abilities, establish a timeframe like "I aim to improve my dribbling skills within the next three months."

Enhanced focus, motivation, and accountability can result from setting SMART goals. When your goals are specific, you know what actions to take. Maintaining this clarity will keep you focused on the task. Achieving measurable goals boosts motivation by providing milestones. Setting attainable goals helps avoid frustration and maintain motivation. When goals are relevant, they help you align your efforts with your values and long-term objectives. Setting goals with deadlines helps keep you focused and prevents procrastination.

We can examine a real-world scenario. Imagine a high school swimmer seeking to enhance their performance. They established a SMART goal of decreasing their 100-meter freestyle time by 2 seconds in the next three months. By establishing this SMART goal, the swimmer has a clear objective, a means of tracking progress, and a source of motivation and concentration.

Another instance involves someone striving for personal development. Their choice is to improve their abilities in public speaking. Their specific goal is to present for 10 minutes at their local community center within six weeks. Setting this goal helps them establish a clear path, monitor their progress, and maintain motivation.

To establish your own SMART objectives:

1. Begin by establishing precise and explicit goals.
2. Clearly state your desired goals and objectives.
3. Ensure your goals are measurable by including criteria for tracking progress.

4. Make sure your goals are achievable and realistic based on your current abilities and resources.
5. Make your goals relevant by aligning them with your values and long-term objectives.
6. Establishing deadlines can enhance focus and create a sense of urgency.

Your focus, motivation, and accountability can be enhanced by setting SMART goals. By providing a clear roadmap, these goals assist in staying on track and achieving objectives. SMART goals can lead athletes to peak performance and individuals to personal growth.

2

TECHNIQUES FOR ENHANCING FOCUS AND CONCENTRATION

Picture yourself at the race's starting line. Cheers are erupting from the crowd; At that moment, everything depends on your ability to stay focused and composed. Techniques like these can help enhance focus and concentration in this situation. In this chapter, we'll delve into techniques for staying focused and rational in both practice and competition. Whether it's mindfulness exercises or pre-performance routines, these techniques ensure optimal performance regardless of the situation.

THE ART OF MINDFULNESS: STAYING PRESENT IN THE MOMENT

At the moment of distraction or judgment, mindfulness is being fully present and engaged. The key is to focus on the present rather than obsessing over the future or dwelling on the past. Mindfulness can revolutionize the game for athletes. By staying present, you can enhance focus and react more effectively in competition, guaranteeing your best performance each time.

Begin your mindfulness journey with simple exercises.

The practice of focused breathing is simple and easy to do. Discover a calm environment, find a cozy position, and relax by closing your eyes. Inhale deeply, allowing the air to fill your lungs, then exhale slowly. Direct all your attention to your breath, noticing each inhalation and exhalation. If you find your thoughts drifting, gently refocus on your breath. The body scan meditation is another exercise that is effective. Find a comfortable position and shut your eyes. Gradually focus your attention on various body parts, beginning with your toes and progressing towards your head. Pay attention to any sensations, tension, or relaxation in every region. This practice helps increase body awareness and can be especially useful for athletes who must tune into their physical state during training and competition.

Another effective method of practicing mindfulness is through mindful observation. While practicing, pause and observe your surroundings without any judgments. Pay attention to the sounds, sights, and smells surrounding you. By doing this exercise, you can stay focused and concentrated in the present moment.

Athletes can experience multiple benefits from practicing mindfulness. Increased focus and concentration are some of the biggest benefits. By practicing mindfulness, you can train your brain to stay focused during practice and competition. Another important advantage is the reduction in stress and anxiety levels. Practicing mindfulness can calm the mind, making it easier to handle pressure and perform well under stress. Your ability to bounce back from mistakes is improved by practicing mindfulness. Rather than fixating on mistakes, you learn to recognize them, release them, and redirect your attention to the task.

Mindfulness has become a part of the training routines of numerous successful athletes. Phil Jackson, the renowned coach of the Chicago Bulls and LA Lakers, employed mindfulness to keep his players focused and present during games. Jackson, known as the "Zen Master," integrated meditation techniques into his coaching, resulting in multiple championship wins for his teams. Another athlete who incorporates mindfulness into their routine is LeBron James. James maintains his calm and focus, both on and off the court, through meditation. His capacity to stay level-headed in stressful situations has aided his success as one of the greatest basketball players of all time.

Practice mindfulness with focused breathing.

1. Find a secluded spot where you won't be bothered.
2. Find a comfortable sitting position with a straight back and hands on your lap.
3. Take a moment to close your eyes and inhale deeply through your nose, allowing the air to fill your lungs.
4. Release any tension by exhaling slowly through your mouth.
5. Pay close attention to your breath, observing each inhalation and exhalation.
6. When your mind starts to drift, gently redirect your attention to your breath.

7. Keep practicing for 5-10 minutes, gradually increasing the duration as you feel more at ease.

By integrating mindfulness into your daily routine, you can greatly enhance your athletic performance and overall well-being. Enhance your ability to recover from mistakes by staying present and focused. Mindfulness can keep you grounded and help you perform your best, whether it's on the field, in the gym, or facing challenges.

VISUALIZATION TECHNIQUES: PICTURING SUCCESS TO ACHIEVE IT

Creating a mental image of what you want to achieve is visualization. Picture yourself in a crucial moment of a game or competition, visualizing every aspect of your triumph. Mentally rehearse your actions, build confidence, and prepare your mind for the experience through visualization. This technique is extremely valuable for athletes. Mentally practicing specific skills or plays and boosting confidence can improve performance through visualizing success.

Visualization can be effectively achieved through guided imagery. To execute this process, you must adhere to a guided script that navigates you through a thorough mental practice of your performance. Guided imagery scripts can be found online or personalized by a coach. For instance, if you play basketball, a guided script could walk you through the steps of making a free throw, starting from approaching the line to experiencing the ball smoothly going through the net. By engaging in this thorough mental rehearsal, you can better prepare for the experience, making it less intimidating and more familiar.

Another effective technique is self-directed visualization. To complete this process, you must envision yourself performing successfully. Locate a peaceful spot where you can be undisturbed, shut your eyes, and envision your own success. Imagine every aspect: the sights, sounds, and smells of the surroundings. Visualize yourself performing with confidence and control, showcasing your skills. This exercise enhances mental preparation and strengthens positive results, increasing your self-assurance.

Incorporating visual aids can improve your visualization exercises. Observing successful performances, whether your own or those of other athletes, can enhance your mental imagery through visual references. For example, gymnasts may observe flawless routines on videos to imagine their own performance, including the same precision and elegance. Soccer players can improve their mental rehearsal by visualizing perfect shots.

Visualization offers athletes significant benefits. By visualizing and mentally rehearsing, you can boost your performance and make it feel more comfortable. By enabling you to envision your own success, it can boost your confidence. By providing a clear mental image of your goals, visualization enhances focus and helps you stay on track during practice and competition.

Take Michael Phelps, an Olympic history-making swimmer, for example. Phelps mentally prepared for his races using detailed visualization techniques. Before bed each night, he would mentally rehearse every detail of his performance, envisioning each step from entering the pool area to finishing the race. By mentally rehearsing, he remained calm, focused, and confident, leading to his remarkable success. Lindsey Vonn, a champion skier, is another athlete who utilized visualization. Before each race, Vonn mentally prepared for her ski runs by visualizing every turn and jump. This exercise improved her anticipation and readiness for all parts of the course, boosting her performance and providing her with a competitive advantage.

Utilize visualization as a powerful tool to accomplish your goals in sports and beyond. When you mentally practice your actions, you prime your mind for success, increasing confidence and enhancing focus. By incorporating visualization techniques like guided imagery, self-directed visualization, or visual aids, you can improve your performance during training.

BREATHING EXERCISES FOR CALM AND FOCUS: TECHNIQUES FOR YOUNG ATHLETES

Picture yourself playing soccer, with the game tied and just one minute remaining. You feel an overwhelming pressure as your heart races. Controlled breathing is your secret weapon in high-pressure moments. The regulation of your nervous system can be improved by practicing controlled breathing, which reduces stress and improves focus. By concentrating on your breath, you can achieve a state of calmness and enhance your performance.

Deep belly breathing, also known as diaphragmatic breathing, is highly effective for young athletes. It may be simple, but it's incredibly powerful. Begin by assuming a comfortable sitting or lying position. Put one hand on your chest and the other on your belly. Inhale slowly and deeply through your nose, letting your abdomen expand as you fill your lungs. Make sure your chest doesn't move. Let your breath out slowly through your mouth, noticing your belly sinking. Keep repeating this process, paying attention to how your belly rises and falls. By using this technique, you can increase your oxygen intake, leading to a calmer mind and enhanced focus.

The 4-7-8 breathing method is another technique that works effectively. Inhale through your nose for four counts, hold for seven, and exhale through your mouth for eight. This pattern aids in reducing your heart rate and inducing relaxation. It's helpful prior to a major competition or during moments of anxiety. Take a moment to find a quiet spot, shut your eyes, and practice this breathing technique for a few minutes. It aids in clearing your mind and getting you ready for the upcoming task.

Athletes can also benefit from utilizing the valuable technique of box breathing. This method is easy - just inhale, hold your breath, exhale, and hold again for the same duration. One way to do it is to breathe in for four seconds, hold for four seconds, breathe out for four seconds, and hold for four seconds. By using this technique, you can create a rhythm to soothe your nervous system and enhance your concentration. It's advantageous to take breaks during a game or match between sets. Through the practice of box breathing, you can develop the ability to remain calm and focused, even in stressful situations.

Athletes can experience numerous benefits from practicing breathing exercises. Practicing controlled breathing improves your ability to remain calm in stressful situations. In high-stakes situations, your body naturally becomes tense. Practicing breathing exercises helps counteract this reaction, enabling you to stay calm and make improved choices. Another important advantage is the enhanced focus and concentration during competition. When you have a calm mind, your focus improves for any task, be it a critical shot or a complicated routine. Anxiety and stress levels can be reduced through breathing exercises. By directing your attention to your breath, you can silence your thoughts and feel more centered, leading to improved performance.

Breathing exercises are a common part of top athletes' routines. Novak Djokovic, a renowned tennis player, employs deep breathing to remain composed and concentrated. Prior to each serve, he breathes deeply to clear his mind and focus on his technique. This practice has contributed to his success on the court.

Before her routine, Olympic gymnast Simone Biles incorporates breathing exercises. By practicing deep, controlled breathing, she can control her anxiety and maintain her concentration, enabling her to perform at her peak.

Adding breathing exercises to your routine can have a big impact. Whether getting ready for a major match or striving to enhance concentration in training, these methods can assist in maintaining a composed, attentive state for optimal performance. By consistently practicing them, you'll discover their value as a crucial component of your athletic arsenal.

CREATING PRE-PERFORMANCE ROUTINES: ESTABLISHING CONSISTENCY AND READINESS

Picture yourself getting ready to enter the field for the most important game of your life. You're feeling nervous and overwhelmed by the pressure. A pre-performance routine can be crucial in this moment—it can boost your preparedness and concentration if followed consistently. Athletes use pre-performance routines to gain control, reduce anxiety, and improve focus. They establish a familiar sequence of actions that prompt your mind and body to prepare for performance, making the transition from practice to competition smoother and more efficient.

Creating a successful pre-performance routine begins by recognizing crucial elements that ready both your body and mind for the upcoming task. Start with warm-up exercises that prepare your muscles and enhance blood circulation. Enhance your confidence and concentration by using techniques like visualization or positive self-talk. It's important to also prioritize equipment checks. Double-check that everything you require is properly set up and working. By using this check, you can avoid last-minute distractions and be fully prepared.

Pre-performance routines rely on consistency for success. Before each practice and competition, make sure to follow your routine. Consistent repetition develops muscle memory and mental conditioning, making the routine second nature. Consistency is key in reinforcing the routine's effectiveness, whether through stretching, listening to a specific playlist, or going through drills.

Another crucial factor is personalization. Customize your routine based on your personal preferences and needs. What may be effective for one athlete may not be effective for another. Discover the activities and sequences that boost your preparedness and confidence. Take, for example, how some athletes use meditative breathing to calm their nerves. On the other hand, some individuals may opt for an energetic warm-up that increases their adrenaline levels.

Pre-performance routines offer significant benefits for athletes. First and foremost, they enhance your feeling of control and preparedness. Understanding the necessary actions before a performance can alleviate pre-competition anxiety and nervousness. This sense of control helps you stay calm and focused, allowing you to concentrate on your performance rather than getting caught up in the surrounding chaos.

Other important advantages include enhanced focus and concentration during performance. By sticking to a routine, you prepare your mind and body to achieve optimal focus and readiness. Your performance is optimized when you are in this mental and physical state.

Numerous successful athletes have developed effective pre-performance routines that contribute to their achievements. Rafael Nadal's well-known pre-match rituals are meticulously performed. From taking a cold shower 45 minutes before a match to placing his drink bottles in specific positions with labels facing a certain way, Nadal's routine helps him maintain focus and control.

These rituals aren't rooted in superstition; they establish a consistent and familiar setting that readies him mentally and physically for competition. Michael Jordan, regarded as one of the all-time greatest basketball players, had specific pre-game routines. Jordan's daily routine involved listening to his preferred music and mentally rehearsing his performance. This routine aided in his mindset development and game preparation.

The examples demonstrate how pre-performance routines can boost athletic performance. Developing a regular and customized routine can decrease anxiety, enhance concentration, and boost your preparedness for tasks. A well-designed pre-performance routine can make a huge difference in high-pressure situations, whether it's a big game or an important practice.

MANAGING DISTRACTIONS: STAYING FOCUSED IN A WORLD FULL OF INTERRUPTIONS

Distractions can arise from any direction during a game or practice. Noise, the audience, and even weather can divert your focus from the task. Picture yourself trying to focus on your tennis serve amidst a noisy crowd's cheers and boos. The noise can be overwhelming.

Staying focused while playing in extreme weather, whether it's scorching heat or pouring rain, can be challenging. Athletes encounter various external distractions, and here are a few examples. It's difficult to deal with internal distractions. Your focus can be disrupted by negative thoughts, self-doubt, and physical discomfort. You might be thinking, "What if I make a mistake?"" or feel the nagging pain from a minor injury. Internal distractions can hinder concentration and performance just like external ones.

To maintain focus, one must employ practical strategies to manage external distractions. Using noise-canceling headphones during warm-ups is an effective method. Creating a quiet environment by blocking external noise can improve focus and mindset. Another strategy is creating a mental "bubble" to block out external noise.

Imagine being encircled by an imperceptible shield that blocks out any distractions. Regardless of the circumstances, this mental imagery can assist you in staying centered and focused. Paying attention to cues or signals from coaches can also be beneficial. By utilizing selective attention, you can ignore distractions and concentrate on your performance.

A unique set of strategies is needed to manage internal distractions. Staying present and reducing internal noise can be achieved through practicing mindfulness. When negative thoughts or self-doubt appear, recognize them without criticism and gently redirect your attention to the present. Another effective tool is positive self-talk. Use positive affirmations to counter negative thoughts. If you think, "I can't do this," replace it with, "I am capable and prepared."

Your focus and confidence can be impacted by this change in internal thoughts. It's also beneficial to create mental cues or triggers to redirect focus. Develop a cue, either mental or physical, to regain focus when it strays, like tapping your foot or taking a deep breath.

Athletes have successfully dealt with distractions to stay focused. Tiger Woods is a perfect illustration. Woods, famous for his unwavering focus, can tune out the noise of the crowd and stay committed to his game. Whether it's the crowd's roar or the click of cameras, he remains unfazed, demonstrating exceptional mental discipline.

Like other athletes, Serena Williams is skilled at handling distractions. During intense matches, she remains completely focused on her game, blocking out all distractions. Her composure and focus have led to numerous victories, establishing her as one of the greatest tennis players of all time.

By utilizing these strategies, you can effectively handle both external and internal distractions, enabling you to stay focused and excel. When faced with a rowdy crowd, unhelpful thoughts, or physical discomfort, these strategies can assist in maintaining focus and composure towards your objectives. By implementing these techniques, you can build the mental strength required to manage distractions and remain focused during training and competition.

THE ROLE OF NUTRITION AND SLEEP IN ENHANCING FOCUS

Your brain relies on proper nutrition for fuel. Picture yourself driving a car with no fuel left. For optimal brain function, your brain requires the correct nutrients. Optimal brain function is enhanced through proper nutrition, providing the necessary energy and nutrients for focus and concentration. Consuming a well-balanced meal provides your brain with glucose, vitamins, and minerals that enhance cognitive function. This dietary plan enhances alertness, accelerates information processing, and sustains focus during training and competitions.

Young athletes need a balanced diet for optimal performance. Make sure to incorporate protein, healthy fats, and complex carbohydrates into your meals. Athletes rely on protein to repair and build muscle. Chicken, fish, eggs, and beans are great for getting protein. Avocados, nuts, and olive oil contain healthy fats that boost brain health and provide sustained energy. Whole grains, fruits, and vegetables are complex carbohydrates that provide the sustained energy necessary for physical activity and mental concentration.

Another crucial aspect is staying hydrated. Maintaining hydration is crucial for cognitive function and performance. Nutrients are transported to cells and waste products are removed by water, which is essential. Fatigue, lack of focus, and reduced performance can result from dehydration. Develop the habit of drinking water throughout the day, especially before, during, and after exercise. Limit intake of sugary drinks and processed foods. Energy spikes can lead to crashes, making it difficult to stay focused and concentrated. Choose natural, whole foods that sustain energy and promote overall well-being.

Like nutrition, sleep is crucial for your brain. Cognitive function, memory consolidation, and overall well-being all depend on getting enough sleep. While you sleep, your brain consolidates the information you've acquired throughout the day. Retaining new skills and knowledge, as well as learning and refining techniques, requires essential sleep. Insufficient sleep can hinder your focus, decision-making, and reaction time, which are all crucial for athletic success.

Start by setting a regular sleep schedule to enhance the quality of your sleep. Set a consistent bedtime and wake-up time every day, including weekends. Getting enough sleep helps regulate your body's internal clock and enhances sleep quality. It's crucial to create an environment that promotes good sleep. Maintain a dark, calm, and quiet atmosphere in your bedroom. Block out light with blackout curtains and eliminate disruptive noises with earplugs or a white noise machine.

Making a conscious effort to reduce screen time before bed can have a big impact. The blue light from devices like phones, tablets, and computers can disrupt melatonin production, affecting sleep. It's best to refrain from using screens for at least one hour before going to bed. Opt for calming pastimes like reading, listening to soothing music, or doing gentle stretches. Engaging in relaxation techniques before bed can enhance the quality of sleep. Deep breathing, progressive muscle relaxation, or guided imagery can all aid in calming your mind and preparing your body for sleep. By practicing these techniques, you can reduce stress and anxiety, resulting in easier sleep initiation and maintenance.

By including healthy eating and regular sleep in your routine, you can improve your focus and concentration. When you nourish your body with the right nutrients and prioritize rest, you lay the groundwork for peak cognitive function and athletic ability. Prioritizing nutrition and sleep is essential for achieving your goals, whether it's for a big game, studying for an exam, or improving your overall well-being.

These strategies will help you improve your focus and concentration. Mental toughness and performance rely on proper nutrition and sufficient sleep. Developing these habits will enhance your preparation for challenges and success in sports and life.

3

OVERCOMING PERFORMANCE ANXIETY

Imagine this scenario: Jenny, a young gymnast, has dedicated months of training for her upcoming competition. While waiting for her turn, her heart races and her hands grow clammy. She feels her stomach turning, unable to rid herself of the overpowering fear of messing up. Jenny, despite practicing for countless hours, is still plagued by performance anxiety. Many athletes experience this feeling frequently. Performance anxiety is the experience of nervousness or fear that can happen before or during an athletic performance. Athletes at all levels, from amateurs to pros, experience nagging doubts at the worst possible times.

The physical symptoms caused by performance anxiety can be difficult to overlook. Picture your heart racing so intensely that it feels like it could explode from your ribcage. A heightened heart rate often indicates performance anxiety. It can make you feel out of control and unable to focus on the task.

Another giveaway is having sweaty and clammy hands. Your body's response to a perceived threat is hindering your ability to hold onto equipment or maintain a steady grip. You may also experience an upset stomach or nausea, causing a queasy feeling. This can be challenging for athletes who rely on their physical well-being to perform.

Simple movements become unsteady due to muscle tension and trembling. The physical symptoms can fuel a harmful cycle, where anxiety thrives on bodily reactions, making the nervousness even stronger.

Performance anxiety can be crippling, both mentally and emotionally. Your mind can become overwhelmed with negative thoughts and self-doubt, hindering your ability to focus on your performance. Thoughts like "I can't handle this" or "What if I mess up?" may cross your mind." These thoughts can spiral out of control, leading to an over-whelming fear of failure.

The fear can be paralyzing, causing a lack of focus on anything except the fear of making a mistake. Another symptom that is commonly experienced is difficulty concen-trating. You lose focus and become unable to stay present and concentrated on the task. Not being able to concentrate can result in mistakes and feelings of dread or panic, making the anxiety worse.

Think about a basketball player with performance anxiety who can't make free throws due to shaky hands. Despite all the practice, his performance suffers due to pressure and anxiety. A gymnast can forget their routine due to over-whelming fear. Anxiety clouds her memory, hindering her ability to remember the practiced sequence of movements.

Due to nervousness, a swimmer may mistakenly start the race by jumping off the block while her mind is filled with anxious thoughts. These examples demonstrate how performance anxiety can hinder even the most prepared athletes.

It's time to investigate these examples further. Consider the basketball player who diligently practices free throws but experiences shaky hands during a game. The ball becomes difficult to hold due to physical symptoms like clammy hands and muscle tension caused by performance anxiety. The mental turmoil of self-doubt and negative thoughts further disrupts his focus, leading to missed shots.

The gymnast experiencing a mental block forgets her routine due to the fear of failure. Her concentration is disrupted by this fear, making it hard to recall the sequence of movements. Anxiety is manifested in the swimmer's false start. Her racing thoughts and heightened nerves result in a costly mistake during the race.

Overcoming performance anxiety starts with understanding its symptoms. Identifying physical signs such as a faster heart rate, sweating, upset stomach, and muscle tension helps you recognize the onset of anxiety. By acknowledging the mental and emotional symptoms, you can address the root causes of your anxiety. By recognizing these indicators, you can create tactics to handle and decrease performance anxiety, leading to improved concentration, self-assurance, and overall performance.

COGNITIVE-BEHAVIORAL TECHNIQUES: CHANGING NEGATIVE THOUGHTS

Performance anxiety can be effectively managed through Cognitive-Behavioral Therapy (CBT). The main focus of CBT is to modify negative thinking patterns to impact behavior and emotions. This therapy helps you identify harmful thoughts that contribute to anxiety and teaches you to replace them with positive ones. Tackling negative thoughts can decrease stress and enhance performance. Performance anxiety worsens significantly due to negative thoughts. Phrases like "I can't do it," "I will fail," and "Everyone is watching me" often make up negative thoughts.

CBT utilizes various techniques to successfully alter negative thoughts. One effective method is thought-stopping. Whenever a negative thought arises, use a mental "stop" command to interrupt it. This technique helps you disrupt negative thoughts and shift your focus to positive or neutral ones. If you find yourself thinking, "I'm going to fail," simply say "stop" and replace it with, "I am ready and capable."

Another effective technique in CBT is cognitive restructuring. It's about changing negative thoughts into positive or neutral ones. Begin by recognizing the negative thought, then question its accuracy. Reflect on whether there is any evidence to back up this idea. Frequently, negative thoughts stem from fear instead of reality. Exchange the negative thought for a more balanced and positive perspective. For example, if you believe, "I never succeed when I'm under pressure," change it to, "I've achieved success in the past and can manage pressure."

Examining the evidence helps challenge negative thoughts in evidence-based thinking. When negative thoughts come up, pause and question if there's any evidence to back them up. By using this technique, you can gain a more objective view of the situation and diminish the influence of negative thoughts. If you believe people are scrutinizing your every move and evaluating your performance, question the validity of this thought. Most people are more concerned with their own activities than with judging you.

Another effective tool in CBT is positive affirmations. Compile a series of positive affirmations to counter and reiterate your negative thoughts. Your affirmations need to be precise and centered around your skills and potential. Such as saying, "I possess strength," or "I am equipped with the abilities and drive to achieve."

Managing performance anxiety can be transformative with CBT techniques. Modifying negative thought patterns can lead to reduced stress, improved focus, and enhanced performance. Consistency and practice are essential for these techniques, but the effort is rewarded with valuable benefits. If you're an athlete, parent, or coach, adding CBT to your routine can help you conquer performance anxiety and achieve success.

THE ROLE OF PARENTS AND COACHES: SUPPORTING WITHOUT PRESSURING

The involvement of parents and coaches is crucial in shaping the experiences of young athletes. Although their intentions are usually good, their actions can sometimes heighten performance anxiety. When parents demand perfection, it can lead to a high-pressure atmosphere where children believe they must meet impossible expectations.

Picture a parent who values winning more than having fun during the game. The child may think that losing means they are failing themselves and their parents. The pressure can turn sports into a chore instead of a passion.

Performance anxiety can also be influenced by coaches. Focusing on winning can imply that only the end result is important. Athletes may become fearful of making mistakes and become cautious due to this message. Athletes may become hesitant to take risks and lose enjoyment of the sport when a coach only focuses on criticizing errors without acknowledging effort. Athletes in this environment prioritize avoiding mistakes over skill improvement and game enjoyment.

To foster a supportive environment, parents ought to prioritize effort and progress rather than outcomes. Acknowledge the small wins and advancements, regardless of the final result. By doing this, we communicate to children that we appreciate their effort and commitment, leading to increased confidence and reduced anxiety. Emotional support and reassurance are just as important. Demonstrate unconditional pride in your child, regardless of their performance, to affirm their inherent worth. The fear of failure can be alleviated with this unwavering support.

Another crucial tactic is to refrain from comparing oneself to other athletes. Each child progresses at their own speed, and placing them against their peers can cause unnecessary stress. Direct your attention to their progress and accomplishments instead. Realistic expectations and goals can have a significant impact as well. Collaborate with your child to establish realistic goals that are both challenging and achievable. By using this method, individuals can develop confidence and track their improvement, minimizing the stress of pursuing perfection.

Coaches can prioritize skill development and effort instead of winning to support their athletes. Athletes can appreciate the worth of their efforts by concentrating on enhancing techniques and strategies, rather than solely on the final score. Another effective strategy is to utilize positive reinforcement and offer constructive feedback. Recognize the hard work and progress made, and offer practical guidance for continued development. Athletes are motivated and feel supported by this approach to keep improving.

It's crucial to establish a safe environment for open communication. Foster an environment where athletes feel safe to express their thoughts and emotions without worrying about being judged. Athletes feel understood and supported through this openness, promoting trust. Fostering team unity and support can further alleviate performance anxiety. Athletes who have a strong bond with their teammates and feel supported are more likely to be confident and less anxious.

Think about a parent who finds joy in small progress. Rather than fixating on the outcome, they commend the effort and growth shown in the game. The child's pride in their hard work is boosted by this positive reinforcement, alleviating the need to constantly win. An environment of support is created by a coach who prioritizes personal bests over winning. The coach boosts athletes' confidence and reduces anxiety through acknowledging personal accomplishments and promoting ongoing progress.

Parents and coaches can create a thriving environment for young athletes by understanding the impact of their actions and using supportive strategies. To reduce performance anxiety, it is crucial to encourage effort, offer emotional support, avoid comparisons, and set realistic goals. Making a significant difference can also be achieved by emphasizing skill development, using positive reinforcement, creating a safe space for communication, and fostering team bonding. Young athletes can reach their full potential and gain confidence when given the right support in their sports.

DESENSITIZATION PRACTICES: FACING YOUR FEARS

Young athletes greatly benefit from desensitization techniques in reducing performance anxiety. Exposing oneself to anxiety-inducing situations is part of the process to decrease the fear response. Athletes can boost confidence and reduce anxiety by confronting fears. Athletes can effectively face their fears through this method, as it breaks down each step into manageable parts.

There are multiple advantages to gradual exposure. It lessens the reaction to fear. Exposing oneself to anxiety-inducing situations helps reduce anxiety levels. It additionally boosts confidence when dealing with anxious situations. With each step, athletes become more confident and better equipped to handle tougher challenges. Athletes learn that their fears can be conquered through this process, as they discover their own abilities.

A structured approach is necessary to implement desensitization. Begin by pinpointing particular fears and triggers for anxiety. It could range from performing in front of a big crowd to successfully executing a skill in a high-pressure situation. Once you recognize the triggers, make a list of anxiety-inducing situations in order of least to most. Start with the least threatening situation and gradually move to more challenging ones. Stay calm by using relaxation techniques like deep breathing or visualization at every stage. It aids in anxiety management and prevents it from becoming overwhelming.

Let's take the case of a tennis player who feels anxious performing in front of big crowds. She started practicing in front of a few friends and accumulated the audience size. Her confidence grows with every successful practice session, and she becomes better at managing her anxiety. She had the ability to compete even in major tournaments. A diver who is scared of high dives begins with lower heights and progresses to higher ones. Through gradual, manageable actions, he grows more at ease with every elevation, lessening anxiety and enhancing his abilities.

Athletes who have tried desensitization techniques can confirm their effectiveness. For instance, a young basketball player might struggle with free throws in high-pressure games. By progressively increasing the level of stress in his practice environments, from an empty gym to practicing with teammates and then performing in front of a small audience, he gains comfort and confidence. Over time, the once-daunting free throw becomes routine, and his performance anxiety diminishes.

There's another example of a young gymnast who is scared to compete in front of judges. She starts by executing her routine in front of her coach, includes a couple of teammates, and rehearses with simulated judges. Every action aids her in anxiety management and confidence building, resulting in enhanced performance during competitions. Through this gradual exposure, she learns that judges don't define her performance abilities.

Desensitization practices extend beyond sports. Desensitization can be applied to different areas of life to overcome anxiety. To illustrate, a student who is afraid of public speaking can begin by rehearsing in front of a mirror, then progress to presenting to a small group of friends, and gradually increase the size of the audience. With time, the fear of public speaking decreases and the student gains confidence in delivering presentations.

Athletes can gain confidence and manage anxiety by practicing desensitization techniques. By using this approach, they gain the ability to confront their fears directly, turning anxiety-inducing situations into chances for personal development.

PERFORMANCE JOURNALS: TRACKING PROGRESS AND ANXIETY LEVELS

Young athletes can experience a significant shift by maintaining a performance journal. It's similar to having a personal mentor who assists in reflecting on experiences, recognizing patterns, and monitoring progress. There are various uses for performance journals. You can record your thoughts, feelings, and performance after practices and competitions. Writing allows you to learn what is effective and what isn't. Self-awareness is vital for managing anxiety and enhancing performance.

Creating a performance journal is an easy task. To start, select either a dedicated notebook or a digital platform that you can use. Your comfort is the priority, so the format can be adjusted as needed. Make a commitment to write after each practice and competition. Building a comprehensive record of your experiences requires consistency. Pay attention to particular elements like your performance, thoughts, emotions, and anxiety levels. After a game, you can reflect on your emotions during crucial moments, effective strategies, and anxiety triggers.

Performance journaling offers tremendous benefits. By promoting better understanding of thoughts and emotions, it enhances self-awareness. By writing about your experiences, you can recognize triggers and patterns that contribute to your anxiety. Developing effective coping strategies starts with this awareness. Monitoring progress and celebrating successes are also benefits of journaling. Reflecting on your entries reveals your progress and accomplishments. Your confidence and motivation can be enhanced by this feeling of achievement.

Here are a few examples that demonstrate the impact of journal entries. During the game today, I experienced a strong sense of focus. The breathing exercises I did before the match kept me calm. I successfully completed three passes and scored a goal. My coach's praise boosted my pride in the effort I put in. Another entry might analyze a high-anxiety situation:

I was feeling nervous and unable to focus during today's practice. I had sweaty hands and constant thoughts of messing up. I attempted deep breathing, but it only provided slight relief. In the future, I'll attempt to integrate breathing and visualization to determine if it improves the outcome.

Your emotional and mental state can be tracked using performance journals. As an example, you may observe that your anxiety is more elevated before significant competitions but remains manageable during regular practices. By acknowledging this pattern, you can concentrate on targeted approaches for handling pre-competition anxiety. Relaxation techniques or positive affirmations could be more effective as well. When you document these findings, you develop a customized guide to handle stress and enhance performance.

Adding a performance journal to your routine can have a transformative effect. It offers a secure environment for you to express your thoughts and emotions, facilitating the processing and learning from your experiences. With time, this habit can decrease anxiety, improve self-awareness, and enhance your performance. Performance journals can greatly improve anxiety management and success for athletes, parents, and coaches.

Interactive Element: Example Journal Entry Prompts

- What were the highlights of today's practice or competition?
- What were your emotions prior to, during, and following the performance?
- Before: How did you cope with anxiety and how effective were your strategies?

- What kind of feedback did you get from coaches or teammates?
- In the future, what areas would you like to prioritize for improvement?

These prompts can help transform your performance journal into a valuable tool for personal development.

BUILDING A SUPPORT NETWORK AROUND YOU

Put yourself in the shoes of an athlete preparing for a major competition. The mounting pressure is causing anxiety to creep in. Similar to these examples, a strong support system can make a huge difference. With a support network, you can receive emotional support, encouragement, and practical advice to help you overcome performance anxiety. It's more than just having people nearby. These people can lend an ear, share their stories, and give you the motivation to keep going.

Parents, coaches, teammates, and mentors are essential members of a support network. Unconditional support and encouragement from parents plays a crucial role. They are typically the ones who notice your anxiety first and can provide comforting words and reassurance. Guidance and positive reinforcement are crucial aspects of coaching. They can help you develop strategies to manage anxiety and improve your performance.

Team members offer companionship and reciprocal assistance. Having supportive teammates can increase confidence and alleviate isolation. Mentors provide valuable guidance and insight. Valuable insights and advice can be provided by someone who has gone through similar experiences.

Effort and communication are necessary for building and maintaining a support network. Begin by reaching out to the members of your support network. Express your emotions, worries, and objectives to them. Building trust and ensuring alignment is facilitated by this transparency. Request constructive feedback and seek advice. Don't be afraid to ask for help or guidance when needed.

New perspectives and improvement can result from constructive feedback. Participating in team-building activities can help build stronger relationships. Group exercises, team outings, and bonding activities can strengthen camaraderie and mutual support. Express your gratitude and appreciation for the support you are given. Maintaining strong relationships can be as easy as saying thank you or showing kindness.

Think about the tale of a swimmer who depended on their teammates for motivation in competitions. The swimmer sought support from their teammates due to pre-race anxiety. The swimmer's nerves were calmed by the encouraging words and shared experiences. The swimmer's performance improved significantly when they felt the support of their teammates. A mentor provided invaluable guidance to a young soccer player. The mentor, who used to be an athlete, discussed their experiences and provided practical tips for dealing with anxiety. The guidance provided the soccer player with effective strategies for maintaining calm and focus in games.

Your ability to handle performance anxiety can be influenced by having a strong support network. Receiving emotional support, encouragement, and practical advice can enhance your confidence and maintain your focus. Every member of your support network, whether it's your parents, coach, teammates, or mentor, has a crucial role to play. You can overcome performance anxiety and reach your goals by establishing a strong support network.

4

BUILDING CONFIDENCE AND SELF-ESTEEM

When Jake first started playing baseball, he was always the smallest player on the team. He often experienced being ignored and doubted his ability to make a significant impact. The coach provided him with a tiny notebook and told him to record one positive aspect of his practice each day. His game started to improve, and, most importantly, so did his confidence. This chapter explores how to build confidence and self-esteem using daily affirmations.

DAILY AFFIRMATIONS: BUILDING A POSITIVE MINDSET

Affirmations are daily statements that counteract negative thoughts. Start your day by declaring, "I can conquer any challenges."

Creating effective affirmations requires thoughtful deliberation. First, use the present tense. Confirming the possession of qualities like confidence or determination increases their power. Next, be specific. Instead of a generic promise, choose to say "I achieve my goals by being dedicated and putting in effort." Avoid negative words or phrases. Swap out "I am not afraid" for "I am filled with courage."

Incorporating affirmations into your daily routine can yield immense advantages. Consistently using affirmations can enhance your mood and perspective. When you start your day with positive statements, you set a positive tone for the rest of the day. Your focus on goals and tasks can be enhanced through affirmations as well. Keeping in mind your strengths and abilities helps you stay motivated and focused on your goals. Affirmations increase resilience and the ability to handle challenges. Affirmations can provide a mental boost when you encounter obstacles, reminding you of your ability to conquer challenges.

Here are some sample affirmations you can use or adapt to fit your needs:

- "I am confident and capable."
- "I am increasing in strength daily."
- "I am focused and determined to succeed."
- "I am powerful enough to conquer and achieve my goals."
- "I am resilient and can handle any challenge."
- "I am proud of my progress and excited about my future."
- "I believe in myself and my abilities."

INTERACTIVE ELEMENT: CRAFT YOUR AFFIRMATIONS

Take a moment to create your affirmations. Here are a few prompts to get you started:

1. Identify a quality you want to enhance (e.g., confidence, resilience, strength, patience).
2. Write a positive statement about this quality in the present tense.
3. Make it specific to your goals or situation.
4. Repeat your affirmations daily, either in the morning or before challenging tasks.

For example, to build confidence, you might write: "I am confident in my abilities and trust myself to succeed." If your goal is to improve resilience, try: "I am strong of overcoming any obstacle."

Integrating daily affirmations into your routine can create a positive mindset that fuels your confidence and self-esteem. This simple yet powerful practice can affect how you approach challenges and pursue your goals. So, start today by crafting your affirmations and seeing their positive impact on your life.

CELEBRATING SMALL WINS: PRIZING ACKNOWLEDGING PROGRESS

Imagine this: You've dedicated months of your life to training, investing countless hours of effort. Your performance today showed a small yet meaningful improvement. Perhaps you increased your speed, lifted more weight, or improved your skill accuracy. Celebrate these small successes. Recognizing small victories supports positive habits and maintains high levels of motivation. Acknowledging even small achievements boosts your dopamine levels. This neurotransmitter boosts your mood and motivation, creating a positive cycle that motivates you to keep progressing.

There are multiple ways to acknowledge and commemorate small victories. A progress journal is an effective strategy to consider. Keep a record of your daily or weekly accomplishments and reflect on your progress. By engaging in this practice, you can monitor your progress and feel accomplished. Another practical tip is to set small and achievable milestones. Take your major goals and break them into smaller, achievable actions. Whenever you achieve one of these milestones, pause and celebrate. The act of rewarding yourself serves as motivation for achieving goals. Whether indulging in something you love or pausing to unwind, these incentives provide positive reinforcement that motivates you to continue and achieve success.

Parents and coaches play a crucial role in celebrating small wins. Their recognition and encouragement can impact an athlete's confidence and motivation. Verbal praise and encouragement are simple yet powerful tools. A few words of acknowledgment can boost an athlete's spirits and reinforce their hard work. Celebratory activities or small rewards can also be practical. Organizing a small celebration, like a team outing or a special treat, can foster a sense of accomplishment and camaraderie. Creating a positive and supportive environment is essential. When athletes feel supported and valued, they are more likely to stay motivated and confident.

Consider the story of a young runner who celebrates personal bests in training. Each time she improves her time, she marks the achievement in her progress journal and rewards herself with a small treat, like her favorite snack. These celebrations keep her motivated and focused on her goals. Another example is a basketball player who acknowledges improvements in specific skills. After mastering a new dribble technique, his coach praises his effort and organizes a fun team activity to celebrate. This recognition boosts his confidence and encourages him to keep working hard.

Celebrating small wins is not just about the immediate joy; it's about building confidence and motivation. Each small win reinforces the belief that hard work and dedication lead to success. This positive reinforcement helps athletes focus on long-term goals, even when the journey gets tough. It also fosters a love for the sport as athletes learn to appreciate their progress and enjoy the improvement process.

Creating a positive cycle of motivation and achievement comes from celebrating small wins. Whether it's by maintaining a progress journal, setting attainable milestones, giving yourself rewards, or receiving support from parents and coaches, these celebrations make a difference. They improve your mood, increase your focus, and strengthen your resilience. Take a moment to recognize your accomplishments and celebrate even the smallest victories. These stepping stones are crucial for achieving success.

ROLE MODELS AND MENTORS: LEARNING FROM THE BEST

Imagine a young athlete looking up at their favorite sports star, dreaming of reaching the same heights one day. Role models and mentors can provide that crucial inspiration and guidance. Role models exemplify the qualities and achievements young athletes aspire to. They show what is possible and set a standard to strive for. Mentors provide personalized guidance and support. They take an active role in helping you navigate challenges and develop your skills. Valuable lessons, inspiration, and practical advice can be provided by both role models and mentors.

When finding role models and mentors, start by looking within your sport. Athletes and coaches who have achieved your goals can inspire you. To learn from their experiences, you can attend sports events, follow their interviews, or read their biographies. By seeking mentorship programs and networking opportunities, you can connect with positive influences. Numerous sports organizations provide mentorship programs that pair experienced athletes and coaches with younger participants. Potential mentors can be found at networking events, workshops, and training camps. It's essential to select individuals who share your values and goals. A mentor who shares your philosophy and approach will offer more meaningful guidance.

There are numerous advantages to learning from role models and mentors. Understanding successful habits and mindsets can lead to transformation. Observing how top athletes train, handle pressure, and recover from setbacks teaches you valuable strategies to use in your own life. Your development can be accelerated with personalized guidance and mentorship. Mentors offer personalized guidance, assist with goal-setting, and provide valuable feedback. Another notable benefit is the creation of a network of positive influences. Creating a nurturing environment for growth involves surrounding yourself with supportive and encouraging people.

Consider the story of Kobe Bryant and his mentorship by Michael Jordan. One of the greatest basketball players, Kobe Bryant, often spoke about how Michael Jordan influenced his career. Jordan's work ethic, competitiveness, and resilience inspired Bryant to adopt similar traits. Their relationship went beyond admiration; Jordan advised and guidance that helped Bryant refine his game and mindset. This mentorship played a crucial role in Bryant's development and success.

Another inspiring example is Simone Biles and her coach, Aimee Boorman. Boorman trained Biles in gymnastics and supported her emotional and mental well-being. This comprehensive mentorship helped Biles become one of the most successful gymnasts in history, demonstrating the profound impact a dedicated mentor can have.

Finding and choosing role models and mentors who align with your values and goals is crucial. A mentor whose philosophy and approach resonate with you will provide more meaningful guidance. Seek mentorship programs and networking opportunities to connect with positive influences. Many sports organizations offer mentorship programs where experienced athletes and coaches guide the younger generation.

Networking events, workshops, and training camps are great places to meet potential mentors. Learning from role models and mentors gives you insights into successful habits and mindsets that can transform your approach. Observing how top athletes train, handle pressure, and bounce back from setbacks teaches you valuable strategies to apply in your own life. Receiving personalized guidance and support from a mentor can speed up your development. Mentors provide tailored advice, help you set realistic goals, and offer constructive feedback. Building a network of positive influences is another significant advantage. Surrounding yourself with people who support and encourage you create a nurturing environment for growth.

Learning from role models and mentors brings many benefits. Gaining insights into successful habits and mindsets can be transformative. When you see how top athletes train, handle pressure, and bounce back from setbacks, you learn valuable strategies to apply in your own life. Receiving personalized guidance and support from a mentor can speed up your development. Mentors provide tailored advice, help you set realistic goals, and offer constructive feedback. Building a network of positive influences is another significant advantage. Surrounding yourself with people who support and encourage you create a nurturing environment for growth.

Consider the story of Kobe Bryant and his mentorship by Michael Jordan. One of the greatest basketball players, Kobe Bryant, often spoke about how Michael Jordan influenced his career. Jordan's work ethic, competitiveness, and resilience inspired Bryant to adopt similar traits. Their relationship went beyond admiration; Jordan advised and guidance that helped Bryant refine his game and mindset. This mentorship played a crucial role in Bryant's development and success.

Another inspiring example is Simone Biles and her coach, Aimee Boorman. Boorman trained Biles in gymnastics and supported her emotional and mental well-being. This comprehensive mentorship helped Biles become one of the most successful gymnasts in history, demonstrating the profound impact a dedicated mentor can have.

Incorporating role models and mentors into your journey as an athlete can provide invaluable guidance and inspiration. Whether you look up to a sports star or seek personalized advice from a mentor, these relationships can enhance your confidence, skills, and overall development. So, take the time to find suitable role models and mentors who align with your goals and values, and watch how their influence can help you grow and succeed.

BODY LANGUAGE AND CONFIDENCE: HOW PHYSICAL ACTIONS AFFECT MENTAL STATE

Picture yourself entering a room with hunched shoulders, lowered gaze, and arms tightly crossed. What is your perception of how others see you? More importantly, how do you perceive yourself? Body language conveys confidence to others and impacts how we see ourselves. Standing tall, maintaining eye contact, and adopting an open posture can differ in how you feel and perform.

When you stand tall with your shoulders back, you send a message of confidence and self-assurance. This simple act can influence your self-perception, making you feel more powerful and in control. Maintaining eye contact is another crucial element. It shows that you are engaged and confident in others and yourself. An open posture, such as keeping your arms relaxed at your sides or using expansive gestures, further enhances this perception. These physical cues change how others see you and how you see yourself.

To boost your confidence through body language, practice power poses. These are expansive postures that can make you feel more confident and assertive. For example, stand with your feet shoulder-width apart, hands on your hips, and chest lifted. This "Wonder Woman" can increase feelings of power and reduce stress. Maintaining good posture is also crucial. Whether sitting or standing, keep your back straight and your shoulders relaxed. Good posture enhances your physical presence and promotes a sense of control and stability. Using gestures that convey confidence, like a firm handshake or open hand movements, can further reinforce your self-assurance.

The psychological benefits of confident body language are substantial. Adopting confident body language can improve mood and performance. Standing tall and making eye contact makes you feel more self-assured and in control. This increased self-assurance reduces stress and anxiety, allowing you to stay calm and focused under pressure. Enhanced performance is a natural outcome of this. When you feel confident and composed, you can concentrate better and perform at your best. The connection between body and mind is powerful, and adjusting your body language can impact your mental state.

Consider the example of Serena Williams. Before she serves, she often stands with a confident stance, shoulders back, and eyes focused. This body language intimidates her opponents and reinforces her confidence and readiness. It's a visual reminder of her strength and capability. Cristiano Ronaldo's body language during matches is a testament to his confidence. Whether it's the way he stands before taking a free kick or his celebratory gestures after scoring, his body language exudes self-assurance and control. This confident demeanor boosts his performance and sets a tone for his team.

VISUALIZATION FOR CONFIDENCE: SEEING YOURSELF SUCCEED

Visualization involves creating a mental image of a successful performance or outcome. Picture yourself at the start of a race, feeling calm and ready, seeing every stride, hearing the crowd, and feeling the finish line under your feet. Visualizing success can help build confidence by mentally rehearsing positive outcomes. This mental practice prepares your mind and body for the event, making success feel familiar and attainable.

To practice effective visualization, begin by locating a quiet, comfortable place where no one will disturb you. Close your eyes and take a few deep breaths to relax. Create a detailed mental image of your successful performance. Engage all your senses: see the environment, hear the sounds, feel the sensations. The more vivid and detailed your visualization, the more powerful it will be. Imagine yourself executing each step flawlessly, feeling confident and in control.

The benefits of visualization for confidence are well-documented. Visualization can improve self-belief, focus, and performance. By mentally rehearsing success, you build a firm belief in your abilities. This self-belief translates into greater confidence during actual performance. Visualization also helps improve focus and concentration. When you have a clear mental picture of your goal, you can stay focused and avoid distractions. Better preparation and readiness are additional benefits. Visualization helps you expect and prepare for challenges, making you feel more ready and capable.

Many athletes use visualization to boost their confidence and achieve success. Michael Phelps, one of the most decorated Olympians, used detailed visualization to prepare for his races. He would visualize every aspect of his performance, from stepping onto the pool deck to touching the wall at the end of the race. This mental rehearsal helped him feel confident and ready, contributing to his remarkable success. A champion skier, Lindsey Vonn, uses visualization to rehearse her routine mentally. Visualizing every turn and jump prepares her mind and body for the race, enhancing her performance and confidence.

THE ROLE OF FEEDBACK: CONSTRUCTIVE CRITICISM VS. DESTRUCTIVE CRITICISM

Feedback can be a powerful growth tool, but its quality varies. Constructive criticism provides detailed and actionable feedback to facilitate improvement. It centers on behavior and performance, providing growth solutions and suggestions. Negative criticism that is vague and demotivating. Instead of focusing on behaviors, it often highlights personal flaws, which prevents people from feeling defeated.

There are a few key strategies to give and receive constructive criticism. When giving feedback, be specific and focus on behavior. For example, instead of saying, "You need to be better," say, "I noticed you struggled with passing accuracy; let's work on some drills to improve that." Offer solutions and suggestions for improvement. This approach helps the individual understand what to do and how to do it. When receiving feedback, listen actively and ask questions. Focus on improvement rather than taking the criticism personally. Constructive criticism is an opportunity for growth, so embrace it with an open mind.

The benefits of constructive criticism for building confidence are significant. Positive, actionable feedback can enhance self-esteem and performance. When you receive specific feedback that helps you improve, you better understand your strengths and areas for growth. This increased self-awareness boosts your confidence and motivation to improve. Constructive criticism also helps build a growth mindset and resilience. By focusing on improvement and learning from feedback, you develop the ability to bounce back from setbacks and continue growing.

Think about the tale of a gymnast who enhanced their routine using precise feedback. The coach gave her precise advice on how to enhance her form and technique. By directing her attention to these aspects, she could improve her performance and develop self-assurance. A soccer player who focused on particular skills after receiving helpful feedback experienced notable progress. His coach provided clear feedback and drills to help him improve his passing accuracy. This guidance helped him develop his skills and boosted his confidence in the field.

VISUALIZATION FOR CONFIDENCE: SEEING YOURSELF SUCCEED

Visualization involves creating a mental image of a successful performance or outcome. Imagine standing on the podium, the crowd cheering, and the medal around your neck. Visualization helps build confidence by rehearsing positive outcomes, making success feel familiar and attainable. This technique prepares your mind for events, helping you stay calm and focused.

To practice effective visualization, begin by finding a quiet, comfortable place where no one will disturb you. Sit or lie down, close your eyes, and take a few deep breaths to relax your body and mind. Once you're relaxed, create a detailed mental image of your success. Picture every aspect of the experience—what you see, hear, and feel. Engage all your senses to make the visualization as vivid as possible. Imagine the environment, the surrounding sounds, the feel of your movements, and the emotions you experience. The more detailed and realistic your visualization will be, the more effective it will be.

Visualization can enhance self-belief and confidence. By seeing yourself succeed in your mind, you believe in your ability to achieve your goals. This mental rehearsal helps to reinforce your self-confidence, making you feel more capable and prepared. Visualization also improves focus and concentration. When you have a clear mental picture of what you want to achieve, you can focus on your goals and avoid distractions. visualization helps with better preparation and readiness for competition. Rehearsing your performance helps you anticipate and address challenges, boosting your confidence on the event day.

Many successful athletes use visualization to boost their confidence and achieve their goals. Michael Phelps, one of the most decorated Olympians of all time, actively visualizes races in great detail. Prior to each competition, Phelps mentally rehearsed every stroke, turn, breath, and his emotions throughout the race. By mentally rehearsing, he maintained calmness, focus, and confidence, leading to his impressive success. Lindsey Vonn, a champion skier, employs visualization as a race preparation technique. She mentally rehearses every turn and jumps on the course, visualizing herself skiing with precision and confidence. This practice helps her feel prepared and boosts her confidence before each race.

Incorporating visualization into your routine can build confidence, improve focus, and enhance your performance. This powerful technique helps you prepare for success, making it feel familiar and attainable. Whether you're an athlete preparing for a competition or someone working towards personal goals, visualization can help you achieve your desired outcomes with confidence and clarity.

THE ROLE OF FEEDBACK: CONSTRUCTIVE CRITICISM VS. DESTRUCTIVE CRITICISM

Imagine you're at practice, and your coach pulls you aside to discuss your performance. How they frame their feedback can make all the difference in how you feel and how you improve. Constructive criticism is feedback that is specific, actionable, and aimed at improvement. It focuses on what you can do better and provides clear steps to help you get there. For instance, a coach might say, "Your footwork during that drill needs work. Try keeping your feet closer together and moving more swiftly." This type of feedback is precise and gives you a simple action plan.

Negative criticism that is vague can be demoralizing. The feedback leaves you feeling worse, with no guidance on how to improve. For instance, you might hear something like, "You make mistakes consistently during the drill."

Being specific is crucial when providing constructive criticism. Instead of making general statements, focus on the specific behavior or skill that needs improvement. Instead of offering general feedback, give specific suggestions for improvement, like "You might want to focus on enhancing your passing accuracy." This method enables the athlete to comprehend necessary modifications and provides a clear route to enhance their skills.

Active listening is necessary to receive constructive criticism. Listen attentively without becoming defensive. Feel free to ask for clarification if needed. As an example, could you demonstrate what you mean by improved footwork? Instead of taking the feedback personally, concentrate on making improvements. Keep in mind that constructive criticism is intended to aid your personal growth. Embrace feedback with an open mind and harness its power for growth.

Constructive criticism has a significant impact on building confidence. Providing constructive feedback can boost self-confidence and improve performance. Receiving specific feedback helps you gain a better understanding of your strengths and areas for growth. Your confidence and motivation to improve get a boost from this heightened self-awareness. Building a growth mindset and resilience is also aided by constructive criticism. When you prioritize improvement and learn from feedback, you build resilience and keep growing.

Think about how a young gymnast enhanced her routine with precise feedback. The coach gave her practical advice on how to enhance her form and technique. By giving attention to these aspects, she could improve her performance and boost her confidence. In the same way, a soccer player who focused on enhancing certain skills after receiving constructive criticism experienced notable progress. His coach provided clear feedback and drills to help him improve his passing accuracy. This guidance enhanced his skills and increased his confidence in the field.

Athletes can experience a significant transformation with constructive criticism. It gives the necessary guidance and feedback to enhance and boost confidence and resilience. Coaches can transform feedback into a growth tool by targeting behaviors and providing practical solutions. Accepting constructive criticism can enhance performance and confidence, whether you're a young athlete receiving feedback or a coach giving it.

Feedback is a crucial component of sports and personal development. The way it's delivered and received can impact growth and confidence. Embracing constructive criticism and using it as a tool for improvement can lead to remarkable progress. As we move forward, we'll explore more strategies to enhance mental toughness and achieve success in sports and life.

5

STRATEGIES FOR RESILIENCE AND COPING WITH SETBACKS

Picture yourself on the starting line of a major race. You're experiencing a mix of excitement and nervousness, your heart racing. Despite your hard training, the fear of potential mishaps remains. Picture yourself tripping and falling during the race, despite being fully prepared. You manage to stand again, but the disappointment is overpowering. Despite being difficult, this moment has the potential to be a valuable learning opportunity. This chapter will delve into the transformative power of embracing failure and learning from mistakes.

EMBRACING FAILURE: LEARNING FROM MISTAKES

Failure is often seen negatively, yet it can be a valuable teacher. Failure offers valuable feedback and chances for personal development. Reflect on the words of Thomas Edison: "I have not failed." I've just found 10,000 ways that won't work." Edison's many attempts before inventing the light bulb are a testament to the power of perseverance and learning from mistakes. Every unsuccessful experiment brought him closer to success, offering valuable insights and lessons.

The ability to redefine failure is an important skill to have. Rather than perceiving failure as an everlasting loss, consider it a momentary obstacle. Changing your perspective can greatly impact how you approach challenges. When faced with a setback, remember it's not the end. It's an opportunity to learn and grow. Another important aspect is the positive interpretation. Instead of perceiving it as a failure, consider it as a valuable lesson. It motivates you to examine failures and find ways to grow, transforming obstacles into opportunities for future achievements.

Embracing failure has several benefits. It increases resilience and determination. You become more resilient when you learn to accept and learn from failure. You develop the determination to keep going, even when things get tough. This resilience is a critical component of mental toughness. Failure also enhances problem-solving skills. Each setback teaches you something new, helping you develop better strategies and solutions. This continuous learning process improves your ability to tackle challenges.

Embracing failure makes you more willing to take risks. When you're not afraid of failing, you're more likely to take on new challenges and push yourself beyond your comfort zone. This willingness to take risks can lead to significant personal growth and achievements.

Consider the story of Michael Jordan, regarded as one of the greatest basketball players ever. Jordan got cut from the varsity basketball team in high school. Instead of allowing this setback to define him, he motivated himself to work harder. He practiced relentlessly, improving his skills and determination. This experience taught him the value of perseverance and resilience. Jordan said, "I've missed over 9,000 shots in my career. I've lost almost 300 games... And that is why I succeed." His journey from being cut from the team to becoming a basketball legend is a powerful example of how embracing failure can lead to incredible success.

Serena Williams, one of the greatest tennis players in history, also faced her share of setbacks. Williams experienced several losses early in her career that could have discouraged her. However, she viewed these losses as growing experiences. She analyzed her mistakes, learned from them, and used the lessons to improve her game. Williams credits her approach to learning from losses for contributing to her successful career. She once said, "I hate losing, but I've learned more from my losses than my victories." This mindset allowed her to turn setbacks into opportunities for growth and achievement.

Embracing failure and learning from mistakes can transform your approach to challenges. It helps you develop resilience, determination, and problem-solving skills. Reframing failure as a temporary setback and interpreting it as a learning opportunity you can turn setbacks into stepping stones for success. Remember, every failure is a chance to learn, grow, and return stronger.

DEVELOPING A RESILIENT MINDSET: TECHNIQUES FOR MENTAL TOUGHNESS

Picture yourself going up against a tough adversary in a game. Your team is facing a deficit and the odds aren't in your favor. In times like these, a resilient mindset can be a game-changer. Being resilient means being able to bounce back from adversity and adapt quickly. It's about resilience and staying motivated in the face of obstacles. Having this mindset is essential for developing mental toughness, enabling athletes to remain calm and composed in high-pressure situations.

Practicing gratitude is a proven method for cultivating a resilient mindset. Focusing on positive aspects and expressing thankfulness can shift your perspective, even in difficult times. Gratitude helps you recognize the good in your life, which can be a powerful motivator. For instance, keeping a gratitude journal where you write three things you're thankful for daily can foster a positive outlook. This practice encourages you to focus on what's going well, even when faced with setbacks.

Setting realistic and achievable goals is another essential strategy. Unrealistic goals can lead to frustration and disappointment, while achievable goals provide a clear path to success. Break down your long-term objectives into smaller, manageable steps. This approach makes it easier to track progress and stay motivated. For example, if you aim to improve your running speed, set a goal to shave a few seconds off your time each week. These minor victories add up and build your confidence.

Building a support network of family, friends, and coaches is also vital. Surrounding yourself with people who believe in you and provide encouragement can boost your resilience. This network offers emotional support, practical advice, and a sense of belonging. Whether it's a parent cheering you on from the sidelines or a coach offering constructive feedback, having a solid support system can help you navigate challenges more effectively. Lean on your support network when things get tough; their encouragement can be a powerful source of strength.

The benefits of a resilient mindset are substantial. It enhances your ability to handle stress and setbacks. Resilience makes you better equipped to stay calm and focused, even when things are unplanned. This ability to manage stress can improve your performance under pressure. Resilience also contributes to greater overall well-being and life satisfaction. By learning to bounce back from adversity, you develop confidence and self-efficacy that extend beyond sports into other areas of your life.

Bethany Hamilton's story is a compelling example. At 13, she lost her arm in a shark attack. Many would have seen this as the end of their surfing career, but not Bethany. Driven by her passion for surfing and an unyielding spirit, she returned to the waves just a month after the attack. Her resilience allowed her to overcome physical and emotional challenges, becoming a professional surfer and an inspiration to many. Hamilton's story highlights how a resilient mindset can help you survive and thrive in adversity.

Developing a resilient mindset is a continuous process. It requires consistent effort and practice, but the rewards are worth it. You can enhance your resilience and mental toughness by focusing on gratitude, setting achievable goals, and building a solid support network. These strategies will help you stay motivated, handle stress more effectively, and achieve greater well-being. Whether you're an athlete facing tough competition or navigating life's challenges, a resilient mindset can empower you to overcome obstacles and reach your full potential.

THE BOUNCE BACK PLAN: STEPS TO RECOVER FROM SETBACKS

Imagine you're an athlete who faced a significant setback—a major injury, a crucial game lost, or a personal challenge that knocked you off your feet. It feels overwhelming, and you may wonder how you'll return to your best form. Now is the right time for a bounce-back plan. A bounce-back plan is a structured approach to recovering from setbacks and returning to optimal performance. It helps you regain confidence and focus after a setback, providing a clear roadmap to guide you through recovery.

To create a bounce-back plan, start by recognizing the setback and its consequences. Understanding the impact, both physically and emotionally, is crucial. Ignoring or downplaying the setback can hinder your recovery. Please take a moment to reflect on the situation and how it has influenced your performance and mindset. This acknowledgment is finding your recovery plan, allowing you to understand the full scope of your challenge.

Next, analyze what went wrong and identify lessons learned. This step involves reviewing the events leading up to the setback, the decisions made, and the outcomes. Ask yourself questions like, "What could I have done differently?" and "What factors contributed to this outcome?" This analysis helps you gain valuable insights and avoid making the same mistakes in the future. It's not about assigning blame, but understanding and learning from the root causes. This process can be enlightening and empowering, giving you the knowledge needed to move forward.

Once you've acknowledged the setback and analyzed the lessons learned, it's time to set specific, actionable steps for recovery. These steps should be clear and achievable, providing a roadmap to guide you back to optimal performance. Break down your recovery goals into smaller, manageable tasks. For example, suppose you're recovering from an injury. In that case, your steps include physical therapy sessions, gradual reintroduction to training, and regular check-ins with medical professionals. Each step should have a clear aim and timeline, helping you track your progress and stay motivated.

Seeking support and guidance from coaches and mentors is another crucial element of a bounce-back plan. Coaches and mentors can provide valuable advice, encouragement, and accountability. They can help you set realistic goals, develop effective strategies, and navigate recovery challenges. Lean on their expertise and experience. Their support can help to help you stay focused and motivated throughout the recovery process. Whether a coach provides technical guidance or a mentor offers emotional support, having a solid support system can make a significant difference.

The benefits of having a bounce-back plan are substantial. It provides an increased sense of control and direction.

Knowing that you have a structured plan in place can reduce feelings of uncertainty and overwhelm. It gives you a clear path to follow, helping you stay focused and motivated. A bounce-back plan also enhances your ability to learn from setbacks and avoid repeating mistakes. By analyzing what went wrong and setting specific steps for improvement, you turn setbacks into valuable learning experiences.

This continuous cycle of learning and improvement builds resilience and mental toughness. A bounce-back plan improves your confidence and readiness for future challenges. Your confidence grows as you progress and achieve your recovery goals, preparing you to face new obstacles with greater assurance.

Consider the story of a runner who suffered a significant injury. Instead of letting it end her career, she developed a detailed bounce-back plan. By acknowledging the impact of the injury, she analyzed her training regimen and identified areas for improvement. With specific recovery goals in mind, she included physical therapy, gradual reintroduction to running, and regular consultations with her coach. With the support of her coach and medical team, she diligently followed her plan. Over time, she regained her strength, improved her technique, and made a successful comeback, even stronger than before.

A basketball player who faced a series of losses also used a bounce-back plan to recover. After several disappointing games, he took time to reflect on his performance, identifying areas for improvement. He set specific goals for his training sessions, focusing on skills that needed enhancement. With guiding his coach, he developed a tailored training program and received regular feedback. This structured approach helped him regain confidence and focus, improving his performance in subsequent games. His bounce-back plan facilitated his recovery and strengthened his resilience and determination.

You can create an effective bounce-back plan by acknowledging setbacks, analyzing lessons learned, setting actionable steps, and seeking support. This structured approach helps you recover more quickly and turning setbacks into opportunities for growth and improvement. Whether you're dealing with an injury, a loss, or any other challenge, a bounce-back plan can guide you back to optimal performance, empowering you to face future obstacles with confidence and resilience.

INSPIRATIONAL ATHLETE STORIES: TALES OF TRIUMPH OVER ADVERSITY

When you think about athletes overcoming significant challenges, specific stories stand out that can inspire anyone facing tough times. Take the story of Kerri Strug, the gymnast who performed a vault on an injured ankle to secure the gold medal for Team USA at the 1996 Olympics. Despite experiencing immense pain and pressure, she persevered and successfully executed her vault, displaying remarkable resilience and determination. Her performance in sports history became iconic, demonstrating the power of mental toughness and grit in achieving extraordinary feats.

Another remarkable example is Derek Redmond, a British sprinter known for his courageous finish at the 1992 Barcelona Olympics. During the 400m semi-final, Redmond tore his hamstring and fell to the ground in agony. Instead of giving up, he got back up and began hobbling towards the finish line. His father rushed onto the track to support him, and together they completed the race. Although he didn't win a medal, Redmond's determination and the emotional support from his father became a powerful lesson in perseverance and prizing a strong support network.

Reflecting on these stories, one lesson becomes clear: persistence and determination are crucial. Strug and Redmond faced situations that could have easily led to giving up. Still, their inner strength and resolve pushed them to continue. This persistence is a reminder that even when circumstances are dire, pushing through can lead to remarkable accomplishments. A positive mindset and resilience also play a significant role. Strug's belief in her ability, despite her injury, and Redmond's refusal to let his torn hamstring define his Olympic experience highlight the power of a positive attitude. These stories show that resilience can turn impossible challenges into defining moments of triumph.

Bethany Hamilton, a professional surfer, faced one of the most terrifying adversities imaginable. At 13, she lost her arm in a shark attack. With unwavering determination and a positive mindset, she returned to surfing just one month after the attack. Hamilton's story is a testament to the power of resilience and a supportive network. She credits her family and faith in helping her stay strong and motivated. Today, she continues to compete and inspire others, proving that nothing can hold you back without the right mindset and support.

These athletes' quotes and reflections add authenticity and inspiration to their stories. Hamilton once said, "I don't need easy. I need a possibility." This reflection encapsulates her approach to overcoming adversity. Finding your sources of inspiration can be extremely motivating. Watching documentaries or reading biographies of successful athletes provides insight into their struggles and triumphs.

Taking part in sports communities and mentorship programs can connect you with inspiring role models and mentors. These connections provide guidance, support, and valuable lessons to help you navigate your challenges. Take the time to seek and connect with these sources of inspiration. Their stories can provide the motivation and perspective needed to overcome your adversities. Whether you watch documentaries, read biographies, or engage with mentors, finding inspiration from others can fuel your determination and resilience.

BUILDING A PERSONAL RESILIENCE TOOLKIT: ESSENTIAL TOOLS AND STRATEGIES

Imagine you're an athlete facing the trials of training and competition. Some days, you feel on top of the world while others you grapple with setbacks. A personal resilience toolkit can help you navigate these challenges. A resilience toolkit is collecting techniques, strategies, and resources that help individuals build and maintain resilience. It provides practical tools for young athletes to handle challenges and setbacks, ensuring they stay focused and motivated.

One essential tool for your resilience toolkit is mindfulness and relaxation techniques. These practices can help you stay calm and focused, even in high-pressure situations. Deep breathing, progressive muscle relaxation, and guided imagery can reduce stress and enhance mental clarity. For instance, practicing deep breathing before a big game can calm your nerves and help you concentrate on your performance. Progressive muscle relaxation involves tensing and then relaxing different muscle groups, which can help reduce physical tension and promote relaxation. Guided imagery, where you visualize a calm and peaceful scene, can also be a powerful way to manage stress and stay focused.

Positive self-talk and affirmations are another crucial component. Positive self-talk and affirmations involve replacing negative thoughts with positive, encouraging statements. When you think, "I can't do this," replace it with, "I am capable and prepared." Positive self-talk can boost your confidence and motivate you, even when things get tough. Writing affirmations and repeating them can reinforce these positive messages. For example, you might start each day by saying, "I am strong, and ready to face any challenge." This practice can shift your mindset and improve your overall outlook.

Goal-setting worksheets and templates are practical tools that help you stay organized and focused on your objectives. These worksheets allow you to break down your long-term goals into smaller, achievable steps. Setting specific, measurable, attainable, relevant, and time-bound (SMART) goals creates a clear roadmap for success. For instance, if your goal is to improve your basketball skills, a goal-setting worksheet might include practicing free throws for 30 minutes daily or working on dribbling drills three times a week. A structured plan keeps you on track and allows you to monitor your progress.

Building a support network of family, friends, and coaches is also vital for resilience. Surrounding yourself with people who believe in you and provide encouragement can boost your resilience. This support network offers emotional support, practical advice, and a sense of belonging. Whether it's a parent cheering you on from the sidelines, a friend offering a listening ear, or a coach providing constructive feedback, having a solid support system can make a significant difference. Lean on your support network when things get tough; their encouragement can be a powerful source of strength.

Practicing the techniques and strategies in your resilience toolkit is crucial for maintaining their effectiveness. Set aside time daily to practice mindfulness, repeat positive affirmations, and review your goals. This consistent practice helps reinforce these habits and makes them a natural part of your routine. Updating the toolkit with new resources and insights is also essential. You may discover new techniques that work well for you as you grow and develop. Incorporate these into your toolkit and adjust your strategies as needed. Reflecting on experiences and adjusting the toolkit based on your learning can also enhance its effectiveness. Review what worked well and didn't, and make necessary adjustments to improve your resilience.

Consider the story of a swimmer who faced a significant setback. After a disappointing season, she used mindfulness and positive self-talk to recover. She practiced deep breathing before each race and repeated affirmations like, "I am strong and capable." These techniques helped her stay calm and focused, leading to improved performance. A gymnast who relied on their support network and goal-setting strategies also found success. After a series of challenging competitions, she set specific goals for her training. She leaned on her coaches and teammates for support. This structured approach helped her regain confidence and resilience, leading to better performance in subsequent competitions.

LONG-TERM PERSPECTIVE: SEEING THE BIGGER PICTURE

Imagine you're a young soccer player with dreams of playing professionally. You're training hard, but setbacks like injuries and tough losses make you question your progress. During these setbacks, maintaining a long-term perspective becomes crucial. A long-term view helps athletes see setbacks as temporary and part of a more extensive journey. It reminds you that each challenge is just one chapter in a much bigger story.

Setting long-term goals and breaking them into smaller, achievable steps is a powerful strategy for cultivating this mindset. For instance, if your goal is to play for a top-tier team, you might start by aiming to become a starter on your current team, then work on improving specific skills like dribbling or shooting. Each small step brings you closer to your larger goal, making the journey manageable and less overwhelming.

Reflecting on past successes and progress is another effective way to maintain a long-term perspective. Reflect on where you started and how far you've come. This reflection can be very motivating, reminding you of your growth and achievements. Keeping a journal to track growth and development over time can also be helpful. Write your goals, milestones, and the lessons you've learned along the way. This journal becomes a tangible record of your progress, offering encouragement and insight during tough times.

The benefits of maintaining a long-term perspective are significant. It reduces stress and anxiety about short-term setbacks. When you view challenges as temporary, they become less daunting. You understand they are just part of the process, not the end of the road. This perspective also increases motivation to persist through challenges. Knowing that each setback is a step towards your goal keeps you pushing forward, even when things get tough. A long-term view leads to greater overall satisfaction and fulfillment. By focusing on long-term growth and development, you find joy in the journey, not just the destination.

Consider the story of a marathon runner who set a long-term goal to qualify for the Boston Marathon. Instead of focusing on this daunting goal, she broke it down into smaller, manageable steps. She started by improving her time in local races, then worked on specific aspects of her training, like endurance and pacing. Over time, she saw steady progress, which kept her motivated and focused. Her long-term perspective helped her navigate setbacks like minor injuries and challenging races, leading to her qualification for the Boston Marathon.

Another example is a tennis player who prioritized long-term development over short-term wins. Early in his career, he faced many losses and struggled with consistency. Instead of getting discouraged, he focused on improving his technique and fitness, setting long-term goals for his development. He kept a journal to track his progress, reflecting on his improvements and the lessons learned from each match. This long-term view helped him stay motivated and resilient, leading to significant improvements in his game and success in major tournaments.

Maintaining a long-term perspective is a powerful tool for athletes and anyone facing challenges. You can stay motivated and resilient by setting long-term goals, reflecting on progress, and keeping a growth mindset. This perspective helps you see setbacks as temporary and part of a more extensive journey, reducing stress and increasing overall fulfillment. Whether aiming for athletic success or personal growth, a long-term view can guide you through challenges and keep you focused on your ultimate goals.

In the next chapter, we'll explore how to integrate these strategies into your daily routine, ensuring that you stay on track and build mental toughness and resilience.

6

HOLISTIC APPROACHES TO MENTAL TOUGHNESS

Sam quickly learned that relying solely on physical training wasn't sufficient to excel in competitive swimming. He observed that his best performances occurred on days when he felt mentally focused and emotionally stable. This realization prompted him to investigate the relationship between physical fitness and mental resilience. This chapter will explore the connection between physical fitness and mental resilience, providing you with practical strategies to incorporate into your routine for overall well-being.

THE ROLE OF PHYSICAL FITNESS IN MENTAL TOUGHNESS

Physical fitness goes beyond muscle building and endurance improvement. Engaging in regular exercise can boost focus and decrease anxiety by releasing endorphins, known as "feel-good" hormones. Physical activities cause the brain to release chemicals that induce relaxation and enhance well-being. This biochemical process enhances your mood and improves mental clarity, making it easier to cope with stress and challenges. Training your body also trains your mind to remain resilient and focused, even when faced with challenges.

Mixing different physical activities can enhance mental resilience. Running, swimming, and cycling are great aerobic exercises that boost cardiovascular health and endurance. They also help clear your mind, providing a mental break from daily stressors. Strength training, including weight lifting and bodyweight exercises, builds muscle and enhances mental discipline. The focus required to lift weights or perform a series of push-ups translates into improved concentration and determination. Flexibility exercises, such as yoga and stretching routines, are just as important. They promote relaxation and stress relief, helping you maintain mental balance. Yoga, in particular, combines physical postures with breathing exercises, fostering a sense of inner peace and mental clarity.

The psychological benefits of physical fitness extend beyond the immediate release of endorphins. Regular physical activity improves mental clarity and concentration. Exercising often makes your brain more adept at processing information and staying focused. This mental sharpness is invaluable during high-pressure situations, whether on the field, in the classroom, or at work. Physical fitness enhances your ability to handle stress and adversity. When you push your body through a challenging workout, you train your mind to persevere through discomfort and challenge. This resilience carries over into other areas of life, helping you stay composed and determined when faced with obstacles.

Physical fitness also plays a significant role in boosting self-confidence and self-esteem. You develop a sense of accomplishment and pride as you see improvements in your physical abilities. This positive reinforcement builds your confidence, encouraging you to take on new challenges and push your limits. This boost in self-esteem can be impactful for young athletes, fostering a positive self-image and a can-do attitude.

Let's consider LeBron James, one of the all-time greatest basketball players. LeBron's well-documented training includes aerobic exercises, strength training, and flexibility routines. He highlights the importance of valuing physical fitness for both his body and mind. LeBron teams up with Calm, an app that incorporates mental fitness into his daily routine. His dedication to both physical and mental fitness has played a role in his on-court success, enabling him to perform at his best even in high-pressure situations.

Serena Williams, an athlete who is also considered iconic, is known for her unwavering commitment to fitness. She follows intense and diverse training routines, ranging from high-intensity interval training to yoga. Serena's dedication to physical well-being has maintained her peak performance and improved her mental resilience. She often speaks about how her physical training helps her stay mentally strong, enabling her to overcome challenges and maintain her focus during competitions.

Making use of these insights can have a big impact on your routine. Whether you're a young athlete or an adult, adding physical fitness to your routine can boost mental resilience and clarity. Begin by doing activities that bring you joy and gradually establish your daily routine. Don't forget, the objective is to exercise both your body and mind.

BALANCED ROUTINES: COMBINING TRAINING, REST, AND MENTAL EXERCISES

Picture Emma, a young athlete, who practices gymnastics every day without taking breaks. Exhaustion takes over, leading to a decline in performance and an increased vulnerability to injuries. Emma's situation emphasizes the importance of prioritizing a well-rounded schedule. Achieving optimal performance and well-being relies on balancing training, rest, and mental exercises. The combination of physical training, rest, and mental exercises promotes holistic development, preparing both body and mind for competition.

To achieve balance, make sure your daily schedule includes all necessary elements. Begin by setting up consistent training sessions and rest days. Training sessions need to be consistent while also allowing for muscle recovery and mental rejuvenation. Make sure to include mental exercises like visualization and mindfulness in your daily routine. These practices help keep your mind sharp and focused, enhancing overall performance.

Make sure to prioritize sleep and find time to relax. Rest is crucial for both physical healing and mental focus. Engaging in activities such as reading or spending time with loved ones helps maintain emotional equilibrium.

Taking proper rest and allowing for recovery helps prevent injuries and overexertion. Allowing your muscles to rest prevents strains and fatigue, which can cause lasting harm. Muscle recovery and growth are also enhanced by rest. While you sleep, your body repairs and strengthens muscles, making you more resilient. Mental clarity and focus are improved through rest. When you're well-rested, your mind becomes sharper, improving your focus during training and competitions.

Take the example of Tom Brady, an iconic quarterback recognized for his comprehensive training and recovery methods. Brady's daily regimen involves intense workouts that prioritize functional strength and recovery methods. By incorporating resistance bands into his strength training, he promotes muscle growth with reduced inflammation compared to conventional weights. He incorporates pliability exercises into his pre and post-workout routines to improve muscle recovery. Brady achieves optimal performance and minimizes injury risk through a balance of intense training and proper recovery. By prioritizing recovery practices such as pre-workout vibration therapy and active warm-ups, he highlights the significance of a holistic approach.

In addition to being one of the greatest gymnasts ever, Simone Biles also highlights the significance of rest and mental well-being. Biles manages to balance her demanding training regimen with sufficient rest. She acknowledges that overexerting herself without adequate rest can result in burnout and physical harm. To maintain her mental and physical well-being, Biles uses relaxation techniques and takes breaks. She achieves peak performance by prioritizing rest and mental well-being.

Begin by organizing your weekly schedule to establish a balanced routine. Set aside dedicated times for training sessions, including rest days. Taking rest days is crucial to recover and prevent burnout. Make sure to include mental exercises like visualization and mindfulness in your everyday schedule. Take a few minutes each day to visualize your goals and practice mindfulness for focus and grounding. Make sure to get sufficient sleep every night. Make your bedroom sleep-friendly by ensuring it is dark, calm, and quiet. Reduce screen usage before bedtime and participate in calming activities to ready your mind for peaceful sleep.

You can establish a well-rounded schedule that supports overall growth by adhering to these principles. Being well-prepared for competition involves balancing training, rest, and mental exercises. This method improves both your performance and well-being. Peak performance requires more than just intense training; it also depends on proper recovery and mental focus.

INTEGRATING MINDFULNESS AND MEDITATION INTO DAILY LIFE

Mindfulness and meditation are effective techniques for staying present and focused, particularly in high-pressure situations. These practices are not just for monks or yoga enthusiasts; they are for anyone looking to improve their mental game. Mindfulness and meditation help athletes stay present and focused, reducing anxiety, improving concentration, and enhancing emotional regulation. Mindfulness practice helps you keep your focus on the present moment, preventing distractions from future worries or past regrets. Whether you're on the field, in the gym, or facing daily stresses, this mental discipline can improve your performance.

To integrate mindfulness and meditation into your daily routine, you don't need to set aside hours of your day. Even a few minutes can make a big difference. A straightforward technique is mindful breathing. Find a quiet place, sit comfortably, and close your eyes. Concentrate on your breath, taking a deep inhale through your nose and exhaling slowly through your mouth. If your mind wanders, gently bring your attention back to your breath. This exercise calms your mind and you can do it anywhere, anytime. Another great method to practice mindfulness is through guided meditation sessions. You can find guided meditations online or through apps that lead you through calming and focusing exercises. These sessions often include visualizations and positive affirmations, helping you build a stronger, more resilient mind.

Body scan meditation is another effective technique. Lie down and close your eyes. Begin by directing your attention to various body parts, starting from your toes and progressing towards your head. Observe any feelings, tightness, or calmness in each region. By practicing this, you can increase your body awareness and alleviate both physical and mental stress. Consistent mindfulness and meditation practice can enhance mental resilience and focus in competitions. By incorporating these practices into your daily routine, you'll discover that remaining calm under pressure becomes effortless. This calmness allows you to make better decisions and perform at your best, even in high-stress situations. Improved focus and concentration are other key benefits.

Mindfulness trains your brain to stay present, which helps you concentrate better on the task. Whether it's executing a complex play or studying for an exam, improved concentration can enhance your performance. There are extra benefits to be gained from improved emotional regulation and stress management. By practicing mindfulness, you can better control your emotions and minimize the impact of stress and anxiety on your performance.

Consider the story of Kobe Bryant, one of the greatest basketball players ever. Kobe started off doubtful of mindfulness but eventually became a committed practitioner, meditating every morning for 10-15 minutes. This practice helped him stay calm and focused, contributing to his success on the court. Novak Djokovic, another top athlete, also uses mindfulness techniques. To maintain focus and equilibrium, he integrates meditation into his everyday schedule. Djokovic's dedication to mindfulness has been instrumental in his ability to excel, even in high-pressure situations.

Incorporating mindfulness and meditation into your daily life can be a game-changer. Start with small, simple practices like mindful breathing or guided meditation sessions. Slowly increase the amount of time you spend doing these exercises as you become more comfortable. The key is consistency. Make mindfulness and meditation a regular part of your routine, and you'll see the benefits in your performance and overall well-being. Whether you're a young athlete aiming for the top or an adult looking to reduce stress and improve focus, these practices can help you build a stronger, more resilient mind.

EMOTIONAL WELL-BEING: TECHNIQUES FOR MANAGING STRESS

Imagine you're about to compete in the finals of a major tournament. Your heart races, your palms sweat, and you can't shake the overwhelming anxiety. Emotional well-being comes into play to help you manage the stress. Managing emotions is crucial for mental toughness and overall performance. When you're emotionally balanced, you can maintain focus and resilience, allowing you to perform at your best. Emotional well-being is essential for keeping your mind clear and calm, even in high-pressure situations. Managing stress and emotions can lead to better performance and overall well-being, making it easier to face challenges head-on.

You have multiple practical techniques available to effectively manage stress. Simple but powerful, deep breathing exercises can make a big difference. When you're feeling overwhelmed, try taking deep breaths by inhaling through your nose and exhaling through your mouth. This method aids in soothing your nervous system and redirecting your attention to the present. Another effective method is progressive muscle relaxation. Begin by tensing and relaxing various muscle groups, starting from your toes and moving up towards your head. Engaging in this exercise can alleviate physical tension and induce relaxation.

Journaling and reflective practices can also be beneficial. Writing your thoughts and feelings helps you process emotions and gain clarity. You can use a journal to document your daily experiences, track your progress, and reflect on your learning. Engaging in hobbies and leisure activities is another great way to manage stress. Whether reading, painting, or playing a musical instrument, finding an activity you enjoy can provide a much-needed mental break and help you recharge.

Establishing a strong support system is crucial for emotional health. Supportive family and friends can have a significant impact. They're there to listen, encourage, and keep you grounded. Effective communication with coaches and teammates is also vital. Creating a positive environment for mutual support is achieved when you feel comfortable expressing your thoughts and concerns. There are times when it is necessary to seek professional support. Engaging with a therapist or counselor can provide useful insights and strategies for handling stress more effectively.

Take into account the case of Michael Phelps, who has openly discussed his battles with mental health. Phelps prioritized therapy and mental well-being, contributing greatly to the toughest times, he stayed focused and resilient, prioritizing his emotional well-being. Naomi Osaka is another athlete who supports raising awareness for mental health. She has openly discussed her battle with anxiety and emphasized the significance of prioritizing her emotional health. The openness of Osaka has inspired and emphasized the importance of mental health in sports.

Incorporating these techniques into your routine can help you manage stress and maintain an emotional balance. Deep breathing exercises, progressive muscle relaxation, and journaling can help you develop effective coping strategies. Engaging in hobbies and building a solid support network enhances your emotional well-being. Remember, taking care of your mental health is as essential as physical training. You can confidently face challenges and perform at your best when emotionally balanced.

NUTRITION FOR MENTAL PERFORMANCE: EATING RIGHT TO THINK RIGHT

Nutrition plays a pivotal role in mental performance. A balanced diet provides the brain with essential nutrients needed for optimal function. Proper nutrition can improve focus, memory, and overall cognitive performance. Imagine trying to concentrate on a complex task while feeling sluggish and unfocused. This scenario underscores the importance of fueling your brain with the right nutrients. When your brain receives the proper nourishment, it functions more efficiently, allowing you to stay sharp and resilient.

Creating a nutrition plan that supports mental and physical performance is crucial for young athletes. Balanced meals should include protein, healthy fats, and complex carbohydrates. Protein is necessary for muscle repair and growth, making it a vital component for athletes. Foods like chicken, fish, eggs, and beans are excellent protein sources. Healthy fats in avocados, nuts, and olive oil support brain health and provide sustained energy. Complex carbohydrates, such as whole grains, fruits, and vegetables, offer steady energy levels and help maintain focus throughout the day. Hydration is equally important.

Staying well-hydrated ensures that your brain and body function optimally. Water is essential for transporting nutrients to cells and removing waste products. Aim to drink water on a regular basis, especially before, during, and after physical activity. Reducing the consumption of sugar and processed foods is also vital. These foods can cause energy spikes followed by crashes, making it challenging to maintain focus and concentration. Opt for natural, whole foods that provide steady energy and support overall health.

Specific nutrients play a significant role in mental performance. Omega-3 fatty acids in fish, flaxseeds, and walnuts are crucial for brain health. They actively support cognitive function and have been linked to improved memory and focus. Antioxidants in fruits and vegetables protect the brain from oxidative stress. They help maintain mental function and overall brain health. B vitamins in whole grains, eggs, and leafy greens are essential for energy production and brain function. They support cognitive processes and help reduce fatigue and mental fog.

Athletes who prioritize nutrition see significant improvements in their mental performance. Tom Brady, known for his meticulous approach to health and fitness, follows a plant-based diet. His nutrition plan includes a variety of whole foods that provide the nutrients needed for peak mental and physical performance. Brady ensures that his brain and body receive the best possible fuel by focusing on a diet rich in fruits, vegetables, whole grains, and lean proteins. This approach supports his physical performance and enhances his mental resilience and focus.

Another iconic athlete, Venus Williams, emphasizes the importance of whole foods and hydration. She incorporates a variety of fruits, vegetables, lean proteins, and healthy fats into her diet. Williams understands proper nutrition is vital to maintaining energy, focus, and well-being. By staying well-hydrated and choosing nutrient-dense foods, she supports her mental and physical performance, allowing her to excel on the court.

Incorporating these dietary recommendations into your routine can enhance your mental performance. Plan balanced meals with protein, healthy fats, and complex carbohydrates. Focus on whole foods and reduce the intake of sugar and processed items. Ensure you stay well-hydrated by drinking water throughout the day. Pay attention to specific nutrients like omega-3 fatty acids, antioxidants, and B vitamins, which are beneficial for cognitive function. By prioritizing nutrition, you can improve your focus, memory, and overall mental resilience, setting the foundation for success in sports and life.

CREATING A MENTAL TOUGHNESS JOURNAL: TRACKING YOUR JOURNEY

Imagine you're an athlete like Maya, a young soccer player aiming to improve her game. Every practice and match brings new experiences and emotions. How can she keep track of her progress and develop the resilience needed to excel? A mental toughness journal can be a powerful tool to help athletes like Maya reflect on their experiences and monitor their growth. Athletes can gain valuable insights into their strengths and weaknesses by documenting their thoughts, feelings, and performances. This self-awareness is crucial for developing mental toughness and achieving long-term success.

Starting a mental toughness journal is simple. First, choose a dedicated notebook or digital platform you can access. This notebook or digital platform will be your space to record your journey, so pick something that feels right for you. Next, commit to writing after practices and competitions. Consistency is key. Make it a habit to jot down your thoughts and reflections, even if it's just for a few minutes each day. Focus on specific aspects, such as your performance, thoughts, emotions, and any challenges you faced. This targeted approach helps you identify patterns and track your progress.

Regular journaling offers many benefits. Foremost, it increases self-awareness and helps you understand your strengths and weaknesses. By reflecting on your experiences, you better understand what works for you and what needs improvement. This self-awareness is the first step toward setting and achieving meaningful goals. Journaling enhances your ability to set and achieve goals. When you write down your objectives and track your progress, you create a roadmap for success. This process keeps you focused and provides a sense of accomplishment as you reach each milestone. The act of journaling itself can be quite motivating. Seeing our growth and progress documented on paper or screen can boost your confidence and inspire you to keep pushing forward.

Let's look at some examples of athletes who have successfully used journaling to build mental toughness. Consider a young runner named Alex. Alex started keeping a journal to track his training sessions and races. He documented his performance, feelings during each run, and any challenges he encountered. Over time, Alex noticed patterns in his training that helped him identify areas for improvement. For instance, he realized he performed better with a balanced breakfast and did a thorough warm-up. This insight allowed him to adjust his routine and improve his performance.

Another example is a gymnast named Lily. Lily used her journal to reflect on her performance and identify areas for improvement. After each practice and competition, she wrote about what went well and what didn't. By doing so, she pinpointed specific skills that needed work and set targeted goals for her training sessions. Lily's journal also became a source of motivation. On tough days, she would look back at entries documenting her progress and remind herself how far she had come.

To get started with your mental toughness journal, here are some practical tips:

1. **Choose Your Medium**: Pick something convenient and enjoyable to use, whether it's a physical notebook or a digital platform.
2. **Make It a Habit**: Set aside a few minutes each day or after every practice and competition to write in your journal. Consistency is crucial for seeing long-term benefits.
3. **Be Specific**: Focus on specific aspects, such as your performance, thoughts, emotions, and any challenges you faced. This targeted approach helps you gain valuable insights.

4. **Reflect and Analyze**: Take the time to reflect on your entries and analyze patterns. What are your strengths? What areas need improvement? Use this information to set and achieve your goals.

5. **Stay Positive**: While it's essential to acknowledge challenges and setbacks, make sure also to celebrate your successes and progress. This balanced approach keeps you motivated and focused on growth.

By incorporating these guidelines into your routine, you can create a mental toughness journal that supports your development as an athlete. Remember, the goal is not just to document your journey, but to use your reflections as a tool for growth and improvement. Your journal can become a powerful ally in building resilience, enhancing self-awareness, and achieving your goals.

7

PARENTAL AND COACHING SUPPORT

Emma, a young soccer player, felt a mix of excitement and intimidation when she joined her local team. Although her parents and coach had good intentions, they struggled to effectively communicate their support and advice. Over time, they discovered the effective communication techniques that were essential to building trust and understanding. The focus of this chapter is on improving communication skills for parents and coaches to create a supportive environment for young athletes.

EFFECTIVE COMMUNICATION: BUILDING TRUST AND UNDERSTANDING

A solid relationship is built through effective communication, especially in sports. Trust and understanding are built when parents and coaches communicate openly, honestly, and respectfully with young athletes. Athletes rely on this trust to feel valued and heard, ultimately affecting their performance and experience. Creating a supportive environment for athletes thrives with open communication. By reducing misunderstandings and enhancing team dynamics, it improves outcomes for all involved.

If you want to enhance your communication skills, begin by practicing active listening. Active listening involves giving the speaker your complete attention and responding with careful consideration. When your child or athlete talks about their experiences, listen without interrupting. Demonstrate your genuine interest by nodding, maintaining eye contact, and providing verbal affirmations such as "I understand" or "Please, continue."

Another effective strategy is to ask open-ended questions. Encourage athletes to articulate their thoughts and emotions instead of relying on yes-or-no questions. Questions like "How did you feel about today's practice? or "What are your thoughts on what went well and what could be improved?"" invite more detailed responses. These discussions offer important perspectives on their experiences and highlight areas where support may be necessary.

It is essential to give feedback that is clear and constructive. When offering feedback, focus on being specific and actionable. Instead of saying, "You need to improve your game," provide concrete suggestions like, "Your passing was good today, but let's work on your footwork to make it even better." This approach helps athletes understand what they can do to improve, making the feedback more effective and less overwhelming.

Using positive language is another crucial aspect of effective communication. Focus on strengths and areas for improvement rather than criticism. For example, instead of saying,

"You always miss the ball," try, "You've improved a lot, and with a bit more practice, you'll get even better at hitting the ball." Positive language boosts confidence and motivation, encouraging athletes to keep working hard.

Empathy plays a significant role in communication. Understanding and acknowledging athletes' emotions can strengthen relationships and support them. Show that you care about their feelings by listening without judgment, validating their emotions, and offering support. For instance, if an athlete is disappointed after a loss, you can acknowledge their feelings by saying, "I can see that you're upset, and it's okay." It's natural to feel this way. Let's talk about what we can learn from this experience."

Consider the story of Coach Mike, who noticed that his team seemed disconnected and unfocused. He held regular team meetings where everyone could share their thoughts and feelings. These meetings fostered open dialogue and made the athletes feel heard and valued. The team's dynamics improved, and they performed better in the field.

Sarah, a parent, practiced active listening during post-game discussions with her daughter. Instead of offering advice, she listened to her daughter's perspective, which helped build trust and understanding. Her daughter felt more supported and motivated to improve.

By incorporating these strategies into your interactions with young athletes, you can build a firm foundation of trust and understanding. Effective communication enhances relationships and creates a supportive environment where athletes feel valued and motivated to achieve their best.

POSITIVE REINFORCEMENT: ENCOURAGING EFFORT AND PROGRESS

Positive reinforcement is a powerful tool in motivating young athletes. It involves rewarding desired behaviors to encourage their repetition. Acknowledging effort and progress with specific compliments boosts motivation, confidence, and performance. Imagine a young gymnast who has been struggling with a particular move. By recognizing her efforts and improvements, you can help her see that her hard work is paying off, even if she hasn't perfected the move yet. This approach makes her feel valued and motivated to keep pushing herself.

There are several effective techniques for providing positive reinforcement. Verbal praise is one of the simplest and most effective methods. When you see an athlete putting in effort or making progress, acknowledge it with specific compliments. Instead of a generic "good job," say, "I noticed how you kept your focus during that drill; that was impressive." This feedback lets the athlete know what they did well, reinforcing the behavior you want to see more of.

Another strategy is using reward systems. Small rewards can celebrate achievements and milestones, providing tangible recognition of hard work. For instance, you might create a system where athletes earn points for various accomplishments, which they can exchange for rewards like extra practice time, a small treat, or even a unique team activity. This system motivates athletes to strive for their best and makes the process fun and engaging.

Public recognition is another powerful form of positive reinforcement. Highlighting accomplishments in team meetings or newsletters can boost an athlete's confidence and motivate others. For example, suppose a swimmer has improved their time. Acknowledging this progress in front of the team can make them feel proud and valued. This public recognition can inspire other athletes to work harder because they know their efforts will receive notice and appreciation.

Encouraging self-reinforcement is also important. Teaching athletes to recognize and celebrate their successes helps them develop internal motivation. Prompt them to reflect on their achievements and acknowledge their progress. You might ask them to keep a journal where they note their accomplishments and feelings about them. This practice helps athletes become more self-aware and fosters a positive mindset.

The benefits of positive reinforcement for young athletes are significant. It increases self-esteem and confidence. Athletes feel more confident in their abilities when they see their efforts being recognized and rewarded. Enhanced motivation to continue working hard is another critical benefit. When athletes see their efforts being recognized and rewarded, they feel more confident in their abilities. This recognition and reward enhances their motivation to continue working hard, creating a cycle of motivation where they are driven to keep improving because they know their hard work is acknowledged. Greater resilience in the face of challenges is also a crucial outcome. When athletes receive positive reinforcement, they learn to value effort and persistence, which helps them bounce back from setbacks.

Consider the story of Jane, a young swimmer who struggled with her times. Her coach praised her for her effort and progress, no matter how small. This recognition boosted Jane's confidence and motivated her to work even harder. Over time, her times improved significantly, and she became one of the top swimmers on her team. Another example is Alex, a soccer player motivated by a reward system. His coach set up a system where players earned points for personal bests and teamwork. Someone could exchange the points for small prizes or privileges. This system kept Alex motivated and focused, leading to noticeable improvements in his performance.

Incorporating positive reinforcement into your interactions with young athletes can create a supportive environment that encourages effort and progress. These techniques boost motivation and confidence and help athletes develop a positive attitude toward hard work and improvement. Positive reinforcement can make a significant difference in an athlete's development and success, whether through verbal praise, reward systems, public recognition, or self-reinforcement.

SETTING REALISTIC EXPECTATIONS: BALANCING CHALLENGE AND SUPPORT

When young athletes like Mia join a new sports team, they come in with dreams and hopes. Yet, success doesn't always come in a straight line. It's important to establish realistic expectations to prevent them from feeling overwhelmed on this journey. Athletes feel capable and motivated when challenge and support are balanced. It's about striking the right balance between challenging and achievable goals.

Realistic expectations start with understanding individual abilities. Each athlete possesses their own strengths and areas to work on. Aligning goals with the athlete's current skill level is essential for parents and coaches. For example, if a young basketball player is still improving their dribbling abilities, aiming to be the team's leading scorer may be unattainable and demoralizing. Concentrate on attainable goals that enhance their confidence and skills, like enhancing their dribbling technique or shooting accuracy.

Encouraging incremental progress is another effective strategy. Rather than expecting perfection overnight, emphasize gradual improvements. Celebrate small wins and recognize the effort put into getting better. This approach helps athletes see that progress is a journey, not a destination. It keeps them motivated and reduces the pressure to achieve immediate results. For example, a gymnast working on a new routine can benefit from mastering one element at a time rather than the entire routine at the same time.

Involving athletes in goal-setting fosters a sense of ownership and motivation. Allow them to have a say in their goals and expectations. This collaborative approach makes them more committed to achieving their objectives. Sit down with them and discuss what they want to achieve and how they plan to get there. This conversation sets realistic goals and empowers them to take charge of their development.

It is essential to be flexible and willing to adjust expectations based on progress and feedback. No one should set goals in stone. If an athlete is struggling, it's important to reassess and change the goals to ensure they remain attainable. This flexibility shows that you understand their challenges and will support them through the difficulties. It helps maintain their motivation and prevents feelings of inadequacy.

Unrealistic expectations can have detrimental effects on young athletes. When expectations are too high, it can lead to increased anxiety, decreased motivation, and feelings of inadequacy. Athletes may doubt their abilities and become discouraged. For instance, a coach who pushes athletes beyond their limits without recognizing their progress can create a high-stress environment. Likewise, a parent who sets unattainable goals based on their desires rather than the child's abilities can cause the child to feel like a failure without really meaning it.

On the flip side, setting expectations too low can also be harmful. It can lead to complacency and a lack of motivation. Athletes may not see the need to put in extra effort if they feel the goals are too easy to achieve. Finding the right balance is critical to fostering a growth mindset and encouraging continuous improvement.

Consider the story of Lily, a young gymnast who steadily improved with incremental goals. Her coach set small, achievable milestones for her to focus on, such as mastering a specific move or improving her flexibility. Lily's confidence grew with each milestone, and she felt more motivated to take on new challenges. Another example is Jake, a basketball player who gained confidence through achievable milestones. His coach worked with him to set realistic goals, such as improving his free throw percentage by a small margin each week. These small successes built on his confidence and motivated him to push his limits.

Parents and coaches can create a supportive environment that encourages growth without overwhelming young athletes by setting realistic expectations. Balancing challenge and support helps athletes develop mental toughness, resilience, and a positive attitude toward their sport. Focusing on gradual improvements and involving athletes in goal-setting fosters a sense of ownership and motivation, leading to long-term success and personal development.

CREATING A POSITIVE ENVIRONMENT: FOSTERING GROWTH AND DEVELOPMENT

Creating a positive environment is crucial for fostering growth and development in young athletes. When athletes feel safe, supported, and motivated, they are more likely to thrive. A supportive and encouraging atmosphere boosts their confidence and enhances their overall well-being. This environment can lead to improved performance and a more fulfilling sports experience. That is the bedrock upon which champions thrive.

One effective way to create a positive environment is by encouraging teamwork and collaboration. When athletes work together and support each other, it promotes a sense of unity and mutual respect. Encourage them to cheer each other on, celebrate victories, and pick each other up after setbacks. Team-building activities, such as group exercises or fun outings, can strengthen these bonds. When athletes see their teammates as allies rather than competitors, it creates a more cohesive and supportive team dynamic.

Another key strategy is to focus on effort and improvement rather than just results. Celebrate the progress athletes make, no matter how small. This approach helps them understand that improvement is a continuous process. Instead of only highlighting wins or high scores, acknowledge the hard work and determination that go into getting better. For example, praise an athlete for their dedication to practice or for mastering a new skill, even if they haven't yet seen success in competition. This focus on effort helps build resilience and a growth mindset.

Providing constructive feedback is essential for helping athletes improve. Offer specific, actionable advice that guides them on how to get better. Instead of vague comments like "Do better next time," give them concrete steps. For instance, if a young basketball player struggles with their shooting technique, provide detailed instructions on adjusting their stance or follow-through. This feedback is more helpful and shows that you genuinely care about their development.

Promoting a growth mindset is another vital component of a positive environment. Encourage athletes to embrace challenges and learn from their mistakes. Teach them that setbacks are opportunities for growth rather than failures. When they face difficulties, help them analyze what went wrong and how they can improve. This mindset fosters resilience and a love for learning, which are valuable qualities in sports and life.

Having positive role models can also inspire and motivate young athletes. Role models exemplify the qualities and behaviors athletes aspire to. Coaches, older teammates, and professional athletes can serve as these role models. Highlight their hard work, determination, and positive attitudes. Share stories of how they overcame obstacles to achieve their goals. Seeing these role models succeed can motivate young athletes to strive for their best and adopt similar qualities.

Consider the story of a volleyball team that emphasizes teamwork and mutual support. The coach fosters a positive environment by encouraging players to support each other on and off the court. They celebrate each other's successes and work together to overcome challenges. This unity has led to improved performance and a stronger team bond. Another example is a track and field coach who celebrates effort and improvement. Instead of only focusing on who finishes first, the coach acknowledges every athlete's progress, whether shaving a few seconds off their time or mastering a new technique. This focus on growth has helped athletes feel more motivated and confident.

Creating a positive environment requires ongoing effort and commitment from parents and coaches. By encouraging teamwork, focusing on effort, providing constructive feedback, promoting a growth mindset, and highlighting positive role models, you can foster an atmosphere where young athletes feel supported and motivated to grow. This supportive environment enhances their athletic performance and contributes to their overall development and well-being.

THE ROLE OF TEAM DYNAMICS: BUILDING A COHESIVE AND SUPPORTIVE TEAM

Positive team dynamics are crucial for creating a cohesive and supportive environment where athletes can thrive. When team members communicate well, trust each other, and collaborate, the entire team's performance improves. Positive dynamics enhance communication, trust, and collaboration. They create an atmosphere where athletes feel connected and committed to common goals.

Coaches can organize team-building activities to promote positive team dynamics, bonding, and collaboration. These activities range from fun outings and games to group exercises to build trust and communication. For example, a scavenger hunt encourages teamwork and problem-solving. These activities help athletes see their teammates as partners rather than competitors, fostering a sense of unity.

Encouraging open communication is another essential strategy. Create opportunities for team members to share their thoughts and feelings. Regular team meetings where everyone can speak up and express their opinions can be very effective. During these meetings, make sure to hear and respect all voices. This open communication builds trust and ensures that everyone feels valued and included.

Setting team goals focusing on collective achievements rather than individual performance is also essential. When athletes work towards shared objectives, they are more likely to support each other and collaborate effectively. For instance, setting a goal to improve the team's overall defense rather than focusing on one player's stats encourages everyone to contribute to the team's success.

Promoting inclusivity is vital for maintaining positive team dynamics. Ensure that all team members feel valued and included, regardless of their skill level or experience. Celebrate everyone's contributions and make sure that no one feels left out. For example, recognize the efforts of bench players who may not get as much playing time but still contribute to the team's success through their support and hard work in practice.

However, negative team dynamics can hinder performance and create a toxic environment. Poor dynamics can lead to decreased motivation, increased conflict, and feelings of isolation among team members. When cliques form within the team, it can lead to a lack of communication and unhealthy competition. For example, suppose a few players dominate the team's social scene. In that case, others may feel excluded and disconnected, impacting their performance and overall experience.

Consider the story of a soccer team that prioritizes teamwork and mutual respect. The coach fosters a positive environment by encouraging players to support each other on and off the field. They celebrate each other's successes and work together to overcome challenges. This unity has led to improved performance and a stronger team bond. Another example is a basketball team that sets and achieves collective goals. Instead of focusing solely on individual achievements, the coach emphasizes working together to achieve team success. This approach has helped the team develop a strong camaraderie and mutual support.

Positive team dynamics are essential for creating an environment where athletes feel connected, supported, and motivated. Coaches can foster a cohesive and supportive team environment by organizing team-building activities, encouraging open communication, setting team goals, and promoting inclusivity. This positive atmosphere enhances performance and creates a more enjoyable and fulfilling experience for all athletes involved.

ADDRESSING BURNOUT: RECOGNIZING AND PREVENTING OVER-TRAINING

Burnout is a state of physical, emotional, and mental exhaustion caused by prolonged stress and over-training. It's common among young athletes who train hard without proper rest and recovery. Imagine pushing yourself to the limit day after day, with little time to recharge. The constant pressure takes its toll, leading to burnout.

The signs of burnout can manifest in various ways. Chronic fatigue is a significant indicator. Even with a restful night's sleep, you may still experience constant fatigue. Frequent injuries are another red flag. When your body doesn't have time to heal, you're more prone to getting hurt. Decreased performance is also standard. You may notice that despite your efforts, your performance is slipping.

Irritability and a lack of motivation can result from emotional burnout. Activities you once enjoyed now feel like a chore. Feelings of depression can creep in, making it hard to find joy in your sport or daily life. Behavioral burnout might lead to withdrawal from activities. You might skip practice or avoiding social events. Changes in eating or sleeping patterns can also occur. You might lose your appetite or have trouble sleeping, exacerbating the problem.

A proactive approach is necessary for preventing and managing burnout. It's essential to prioritize rest and recovery. Make sure to incorporate regular rest days and breaks into your schedule for your body and mind to recover. While it may be tempting to believe that more training yields better results, resting is crucial to prevent burnout. It is crucial to also encourage a well-rounded schedule. Emphasize a combination of physical activity, rest, and diverse pastimes. Engage in hobbies outside of sports to keep your life well-rounded and enjoyable.

Monitoring training intensity helps prevent over-training. It is crucial to adapt training loads according to the athlete's condition and feedback. When athletes feel tired or stressed, it's important to reduce the intensity or duration of their workouts.

Providing emotional support is essential. Show empathy and understanding, while promoting open communication. Let athletes know that it's okay to express their feelings and concerns. Knowing that someone is listening can make a big difference. Share stories of athletes who have managed burnout.

For example, consider a swimmer who adjusted their training schedule to prevent burnout. After recognizing the signs of exhaustion, they worked with their coach to create a more balanced routine, incorporating more rest days and lighter training sessions. This change improved their performance and restored their love for the sport. Another example is a gymnast incorporating more rest into their routine. By prioritizing self-care and mental well-being, they recovered from burnout and regained their enthusiasm for gymnastics.

The key to addressing burnout is to strike a sustainable balance between training and recovery. Long-term well-being and performance rely on its importance. By recognizing the signs and taking proactive steps to prevent burnout, you can help young athletes stay healthy, motivated, and passionate about their sport.

As we wrap up this chapter, remember that supporting young athletes involves more than physical training. It's about creating an environment where they can grow, thrive, and enjoy their journey in sports. In the next chapter, we'll explore long-term personal growth and resilience strategies, helping athletes develop skills that will serve them throughout their lives.

8

LONG-TERM STRATEGIES FOR PERSONAL GROWTH

When Emma decided to take piano lessons at age 35, she didn't realize how much it would change her life. She thought it would be a fun hobby, but it became a powerful tool for personal growth. Each new piece she learned challenged her mind, improved her focus, and made her more resilient. Emma's experience highlights the transformative power of lifelong learning. In this chapter, we'll explore how continuous learning can help you develop mental toughness and grow as an individual.

LIFELONG LEARNING: CONTINUOUSLY DEVELOPING MENTAL SKILLS

Lifelong learning is a commitment to constantly expanding your knowledge and skills. It's about staying curious, open-minded, and willing to learn new things, regardless of your age or stage. This commitment to continuous learning contributes significantly to mental toughness and personal growth. Lifelong learning helps individuals adapt to new challenges and stay mentally sharp. It keeps your brain active, crucial for maintaining cognitive function as you age. Continuous learning enhances problem-solving skills, creativity, and resilience. When you seek new knowledge and experiences, you develop a more flexible and adaptable mindset, which allows you to navigate life's challenges more effectively.

One of the most practical ways to integrate lifelong learning into your daily life is reading books and articles on topics that interest you. Whether it's a biography of a renowned athlete, a book on mental toughness, or articles on the latest advancements in your field, reading keeps you informed and inspired. Taking online courses or attending workshops is another excellent strategy. Many platforms offer classes on various subjects, allowing you to learn at your own pace and convenience.

Workshops provide hands-on experience and the opportunity to interact with experts and peers, enhancing your learning experience. Seeking new experiences and challenges is also essential. Trying recent activities, traveling to new places, and meeting new people can broaden your horizons and stimulate your mind. Discussions and debates can further deepen your understanding and encourage critical thinking. These conversations can expose you to different perspectives and ideas, helping you grow mentally and emotionally.

Embracing a growth mindset is a critical component of life-long learning. Embracing a growth mindset means that individuals believe they can develop their abilities through effort, knowledge, and persistence. This mindset supports continuous development by increasing your willingness to take on new challenges. When you believe you can improve, you're more likely to push yourself out of your comfort zone and persist in facing obstacles. A growth mindset also enhances your ability to learn from mistakes. Instead of seeing failures as setbacks, you view them as opportunities to grow and improve. This perspective fosters resilience and helps you bounce back stronger from difficulties.

Consider the story of Sarah, a professional athlete who pursued further education while training for competitions. Despite her demanding schedule, she enrolled in online courses related to sports psychology. Sarah found that the knowledge she gained improved her performance and gave her a deeper understanding of her mental processes. This continuous learning helped her stay sharp and adaptable on and off the field.

Another example is Mark, a software engineer who regularly attends workshops and seminars to stay updated in his field. Mark's dedication to learning has enabled him to stay ahead of industry trends and enhance his skills. His proactive approach to education has made him a valuable asset to his team and has opened up new career opportunities.

Interactive Element: Lifelong Learning Action Plan

Create your own lifelong learning action plan with these steps:

1. **Identify Your Interests**: List topics or skills you want to learn more about.
2. **Set Learning Goals**: Decide what you want to achieve in the next month, six months, and a year.

3. **Find Resources**: Look for books, online courses, workshops, and other learning materials related to your interests.
4. **Schedule Learning Time**: Dedicate specific times each week to focus on learning.
5. **Reflect on Your Progress**: Regularly review what you've learned and how it has impacted your personal and professional life.

By incorporating these strategies into your routine, you can foster a habit of lifelong learning that will develop your mental skills and contribute to your personal growth.

MAINTAINING MOTIVATION: STRATEGIES FOR CONSISTENT EFFORT

Imagine you're running a marathon. You are excited and energetic at the outset, but the real challenge comes midway when fatigue sets in. The midway stage is where maintaining motivation becomes crucial. Sustained motivation helps you stay committed to your goals and sustain progress. The driving force keeps you moving forward, even when the initial excitement has worn off. Consistent effort leads to continuous improvement and achievement, making motivation a key component of long-term success and personal growth.

Setting both short-term and long-term goals is a powerful way to maintain motivation. Short-term goals provide immediate targets to aim for, keeping you engaged and focused. They act as stepping stones towards your larger objectives. Long-term goals, however, give you a clear vision of what you want to achieve in the bigger picture. For instance, if you're a young athlete, a short-term goal might improve your sprint time, while a long-term goal could earn a college scholarship. Celebrating small wins and milestones along the way keeps you motivated by acknowledging your progress. Each small victory reminds you that you're moving in the right direction, reinforcing your commitment to your larger goals.

Finding intrinsic motivation is another essential strategy. Intrinsic motivation comes from within—connecting your goals to your values and passions. Staying motivated becomes much easier when you pursue something that matters to you. For example, if you love playing soccer because it brings you joy and a sense of accomplishment, that intrinsic motivation will keep you going during tough training sessions. Seeking inspiration from role models and mentors can also boost your motivation. Observing the dedication and perseverance of others can inspire you to stay committed to your goals. Role models provide a tangible example of what's possible. Mentors offer guidance and support, helping you navigate challenges and stay focused.

Self-discipline plays a vital role in maintaining motivation. It helps you stay focused and avoid distractions, ensuring you continue progressing towards your goals. Creating a structured routine is one way to build self-discipline. A consistent schedule helps you develop good habits and reduces the temptation to procrastinate. Setting boundaries is also essential. For instance, allocating specific times for training, studying, or working helps you prioritize your tasks and stay on track. Holding yourself accountable is another crucial aspect of self-discipline. Setting boundaries could involve reviewing your goals, tracking your progress, and adjusting as needed. Holding yourself accountable makes you more likely to stay committed and motivated.

Consider the story of Emily, a marathon runner who stayed motivated through daily training. Emily set clear short-term goals, such as improving her pace, and celebrated each milestone she achieved. Her intrinsic motivation came from her love of running and the freedom it gave her. She also drew inspiration from elite marathoners, whose perseverance stories fueled her determination. Emily created a structured routine, waking up early every morning to train, and held herself accountable by tracking her progress in a journal. Her consistent effort and self-discipline paid off, and she completed multiple marathons, improving her performance.

Then there's Alex, an entrepreneur who faced many setbacks in his business. Despite the challenges, Alex maintained his motivation by setting short-term and long-term goals. He celebrated small wins, like securing a new client or launching a new product, which kept his spirits high. Alex's intrinsic motivation came from his passion for innovation and desire to impact the lives of others. He sought inspiration from successful entrepreneurs and mentors who provided valuable advice and encouragement. Alex practiced self-discipline by maintaining a structured routine and holding himself accountable for his progress. His consistent effort and dedication helped him overcome obstacles and achieve significant growth in his business.

Maintaining motivation is essential for long-term success and personal growth. By setting clear goals, celebrating milestones, finding intrinsic motivation, seeking inspiration, and practicing self-discipline, you can keep your motivation high and achieve your objectives. Whether you're an athlete aiming for peak performance or an individual pursuing personal or professional goals, these strategies will help you stay committed and improve.

ADAPTING TO LIFE CHANGES: FLEXIBILITY AND MENTAL TOUGHNESS

Life is full of unexpected twists and turns. Picture this: you're a seasoned athlete, and an injury forces you to reconsider your entire career. This scenario might sound daunting, but it highlights the importance of flexibility and adaptability. Being flexible allows you to navigate changes and challenges. Adaptability enhances resilience, problem-solving skills, and overall well-being. When you can adjust to new circumstances, you build mental toughness that helps you overcome adversity and thrive in various aspects of life.

Embracing change as an opportunity for growth is a powerful strategy for developing flexibility. Instead of fearing the unknown, view changes as chances to learn and improve. This mindset shift can transform challenges into valuable experiences that contribute to your growth. Practicing mindfulness and staying present also play crucial roles in becoming more adaptable. Mindfulness helps you stay grounded and focused, making it easier to handle sudden changes without feeling overwhelmed. When present, you can assess situations more clearly and respond thoughtfully, rather than impulsively.

Developing problem-solving skills and creative thinking further enhances your adaptability. When faced with a challenge, approach it with curiosity and an open mind. Brainstorm different solutions, weigh the pros and cons, and choose the best action. This proactive approach builds your confidence in handling uncertainties. Seeking support from friends, family, and mentors is equally essential. Surrounding yourself with a strong support network provides emotional stability and practical advice. These relationships offer different perspectives and insights that can help you navigate changes more effectively.

A flexible mindset brings numerous benefits. It increases your resilience and ability to handle stress. When you're open to change, you become more adept at returning from setbacks. This resilience is crucial for maintaining mental toughness. Additionally, flexibility enhances your ability to learn and grow from new experiences. Each change becomes an opportunity to gain new skills and knowledge, contributing to your overall development. This openness to learning leads to greater satisfaction and fulfillment in life. When you embrace new experiences, you enrich your life with diverse perspectives and opportunities.

Consider the story of Maria, a professional gymnast who faced a career-ending injury. Instead of seeing this as the end of her journey, she viewed it as an opportunity to explore new paths. Maria transitioned to coaching and mentoring young athletes through her experience and skills. Her adaptability allowed her to find a new sense of purpose and fulfillment. Another example is John, a marketing executive who had to adapt to rapid changes in his industry. John successfully navigated the shift to digital marketing by staying flexible and continuously learning. He embraced new technologies and strategies, ensuring relevance and success in a changing market.

Flexibility is not just about adapting to external changes; it's also about being open to internal growth. Reflect on your experiences and identify areas where you can improve. This self-awareness helps you recognize patterns and make better decisions in the future. For instance, if you notice that you tend to resist change, work on building a more open mindset. Challenge yourself to step out of your comfort zone and embrace new opportunities. This practice will gradually enhance your adaptability and mental toughness.

To develop flexibility and resilience, integrate these strategies into your everyday routine. Embrace changes as opportunities for growth, practice mindfulness to stay present, develop problem-solving skills, and seek support from your network. As you cultivate a flexible mindset, you'll be better equipped to handle life's challenges and thrive in new environments.

THE IMPORTANCE OF REFLECTION: LEARNING FROM YOUR JOURNEY

Reflection is like looking into a mirror, but instead of seeing your physical self, you see your thoughts, experiences, and lessons learned. Reflecting on your experiences and progress can contribute to personal growth and mental toughness. Taking the time to pause and think about what you've been through helps you gain insights, recognize patterns, and make informed decisions about your future actions. Reflecting enhances your self-awareness, which is crucial for understanding your strengths and weaknesses. This understanding allows you to leverage your strengths and work on areas that need improvement.

One practical way to incorporate reflection into your daily life is by journaling. Writing your thoughts, experiences, and lessons learned provides a tangible record you can refer to. It helps you track your progress and identify recurring themes or patterns. Setting aside regular time for self-reflection is also essential. Self-reflection could be a few minutes at the end of each day or a dedicated time each week. During this time, ask yourself reflective questions such as, "What went well today? What could be improved? What did I learn?" These questions encourage you to think critically about your experiences and extract valuable lessons from them.

The benefits of learning from reflection are many. Increased self-awareness helps you understand your strengths and weaknesses better. This understanding allows you to set more realistic and achievable goals. Reflecting on your experiences also enhances your ability to set and achieve goals. By reviewing your progress, you can adjust your strategies and stay on track. Reflection provides a greater sense of accomplishment and motivation. Seeing how far you've come boosts your confidence and encourages you to keep.

Consider the story of Coach Lisa, who regularly reflects on her team's performance and strategies. After each game, she reviews what went well and what could be improved. She involves her team in this process, encouraging them to share their thoughts and insights. This practice helps the team learn and grow and fosters a culture of continuous improvement. By reflecting on their performance, the team can identify areas for growth and celebrate their successes, strengthening their resolve and unity.

Another example is James, an entrepreneur who uses reflection to learn from his business successes and failures. After each project, James dedicates time to analyzing what worked and what didn't. He keeps a detailed journal where he documents his observations and insights. This practice helps him refine his strategies and avoid repeating past mistakes. By learning from his experiences, James has grown his business and achieved tremendous success. His commitment to reflection has made him more adaptable and resilient in facing challenges.

Textual Element: Reflective Journaling Prompts

Here are some prompts to help you get started with reflective journaling:

1. **Daily Reflection**: What went well today? What challenges did I face, and how did I overcome them?
2. **Weekly Review**: What were my most significant achievements this week? What lessons did I learn from any setbacks?
3. **Monthly Insight**: How have I grown or changed over the past month? What new skills or knowledge have I gained?
4. **Goal Assessment**: Am I on track to achieve my goals? What adjustments do I need to make?

Incorporating these prompts into your journaling routine can help you deepen your reflection and gain more valuable insights from your experiences.

Reflection is not just about looking back; it's also about looking forward. By understanding your experiences, you can make more informed decisions about your future. This continuous cycle of reflection and learning helps you grow and develop personally and professionally. Whether you're an athlete aiming for peak performance, a professional seeking career advancement, or anyone looking to improve, regular reflection can provide the insights and motivation you need to succeed.

FUTURE PLANNING: SETTING GOALS BEYOND SPORTS

Imagine you're an athlete who has spent years honing your skills and competing at the highest levels. While sports have been a significant part of your life, there comes a point when you must think about the future beyond the playing field. Future planning is crucial because it helps you envision your desired future and take proactive steps to achieve it. Setting goals beyond sports fosters a sense of purpose and direction, ensuring your transition from athletics to other pursuits is smooth and fulfilling. It provides a roadmap for personal growth and long-term satisfaction.

Identifying your values and passions is the first step in setting future goals. Understanding what matters to you can guide your decisions and help you focus on goals that align with your values. For instance, if you are passionate about helping others, consider a coaching or community service career. Next, apply the SMART criteria to your goals: make them Specific, Measurable, Achievable, Relevant, and Time-bound. This approach ensures that your goals are clear and attainable. For example, instead of setting a vague goal like "I want to help people," specify it as "I want to become a certified coach within two years."

Creating an action plan with clear steps and milestones is essential for achieving your goals. Break down your long-term objectives into smaller, manageable tasks to tackle one step at a time. This method keeps you focused and motivated. For instance, if your goal is to open a business, your action plan might include market research, writing a business plan, securing funding, and launching your product or service. Seeking guidance from mentors and role models can also be beneficial. Their experience and insights can provide valuable advice and support as you achieve your goals.

Pursuing goals in different areas of life can lead to a well-rounded and fulfilling life. Having diverse goals enhances personal and professional growth, giving you a greater sense of balance and satisfaction. It also increases your resilience and adaptability as you develop skills and knowledge in various domains. For example, an athlete who sets goals in education, career, and community involvement can build a rich and varied life beyond sports. This approach ensures that you're not defined by your athletic achievements, but also by your contributions to other areas.

Consider the story of Mark, a retired basketball player who pursued a career in coaching. After years of playing professionally, Mark realized he wanted to share his knowledge and passion for the game with young athletes. He set a goal to become a certified coach and worked diligently to achieve it. Today, Mark runs a successful coaching business and mentors aspiring athletes, finding immense fulfillment in his new career. Another example is Sarah, an athlete who used her platform to advocate for social causes. Passionate about mental health, Sarah set a goal to raise awareness and support for mental health initiatives. She collaborated with organizations, organized events, and used her influence to make a positive impact. People widely recognize Sarah's efforts, and she inspires others through her advocacy work.

Future planning is not just about setting career goals. It also involves personal development, relationships, and community involvement. For instance, you might set goals to improve your health, build stronger relationships with family and friends, or volunteer in your community. These goals contribute to a well-rounded and fulfilling life, ensuring you continue growing and thriving in various aspects of life. Planning for the future helps you take control of your life and make informed decisions that align with your values and aspirations.

Focusing on future planning ensures that your transition from sports to other pursuits is smooth and fulfilling. Setting clear, achievable goals, creating an action plan, and seeking guidance from mentors will help you navigate this transition successfully. Pursuing diverse goals will lead to a well-rounded and satisfying life, enhancing your personal and professional growth. Whether you aspire to start a new career, contribute to your community, or pursue individual passions, future planning will provide the direction and purpose you need to achieve your long-term objectives.

LEGACY OF MENTAL TOUGHNESS: PASSING ON THE LESSONS LEARNED

Leaving a legacy isn't just about achieving great things; it's about sharing your knowledge, experiences, and values with others so they can benefit from your journey. When you pass on your lessons, you inspire and empower others to develop their mental toughness. Think of it as planting seeds that will grow into strong, resilient individuals who can confidently face life's challenges.

Mentoring young athletes or individuals is one effective way to pass on these lessons. As a mentor, you provide guidance, support, and wisdom from your experiences. This relationship can be impactful, offering the mentee a roadmap based on real-life experiences. Writing articles, books, or blogs is another excellent way to share your insights. These written works can reach a broader audience, providing valuable lessons to those who may not learn from you. Giving talks or workshops on mental toughness allows you to share your story and strategies more effectively, engaging with your audience and answering their questions. Leading by example and showing mental toughness in your daily life can inspire those around you. Actions often speak louder than words, and living out the principles of mental toughness can motivate others to do the same.

The impact of leaving a legacy of mental toughness can create a positive ripple effect in the community. When you share your lessons, you inspire others to pursue their goals and overcome challenges. This inspiration can lead to developing a supportive and resilient community where individuals uplift and motivate each other. Furthermore, by passing on these lessons, you create a lasting impact on future generations. The values and knowledge you impart can continue to influence and shape individuals long after you're gone, ensuring that your legacy lives on.

Consider the story of Coach Mike, who dedicated his career to mentoring young athletes. He didn't just teach them the skills needed for their sport; he instilled in them the importance of mental toughness, resilience, and a positive mindset. Many of his former athletes achieved great success in sports and their personal lives. They often credit Coach Mike's teachings as a significant factor in their achievements.

Another example is Lisa, a retired athlete who faced many challenges throughout her career. After retiring, she became an advocate for mental health and resilience. She shared her story through talks and workshops, reaching countless individuals who found strength and inspiration in her words. Lisa's efforts have helped many people develop the mental toughness needed to face their challenges, creating a lasting impact on her community.

By embracing the concept of leaving a legacy, you ensure that your experiences and lessons continue to benefit others. Whether through mentoring, writing, speaking, or leading by example, your efforts can inspire and empower individuals to develop their mental toughness. Leaving a legacy enriches their lives and contributes to building a more resilient and supportive community.

CONCLUSION

As we wrap up this journey, we must reflect on the key lessons we've explored. We've delved into the importance of mental toughness and how it can shape your athletic performance and your life. From understanding mental toughness to building resilience and learning to cope with setbacks, we've covered a comprehensive roadmap for success.

Throughout the chapters, we've seen that mental toughness isn't just about being strong but intelligent, adaptable, and persistent. We started by understanding the foundation of mental toughness and exploring how focus, resilience, and emotional regulation can transform your approach to challenges. We then moved on to specific techniques like mindfulness, visualization, and breathing exercises, which are invaluable tools for enhancing your focus and concentration.

Next, we tackled performance anxiety and discovered practical ways to manage it, such as cognitive-behavioral techniques and the importance of a supportive network. Building confidence and self-esteem through daily affirmations, celebrating small wins, and finding role models have also been crucial to our discussion. We've seen how setting SMART goals and maintaining a balance between training, rest, and mental exercises can lead to holistic development.

Resilience and coping with setbacks were significant themes, too. Embracing failure, developing a resilient mindset, and having a bounce-back plan are all strategies that can turn challenges into opportunities. We've shared stories of athletes who have triumphed over adversity, showing that mental toughness is a skill anyone can develop.

In exploring holistic approaches, we discussed the significant role of physical fitness, balanced routines, and nutrition in building mental toughness. We also emphasized the value of emotional well-being and the creation of a personal resilience toolkit. The support of parents and coaches, effective communication, and preventing burnout are all critical elements in fostering a positive environment for young athletes.

Finally, we looked at long-term strategies for personal growth, including lifelong learning, maintaining motivation, adapting to life changes, and planning for the future beyond sports. Leaving a legacy of mental toughness by passing on the lessons learned is a powerful way to make a lasting impact.

So, what are the key takeaways? First, mental toughness is a journey, not a destination. It involves continuous learning, self-reflection, and the willingness to embrace challenges. Second, building a support network of parents, coaches, and peers is crucial. They provide the encouragement and guidance needed to navigate the highs and lows. Third, practical techniques like mindfulness, visualization, and positive self-talk are invaluable tools for enhancing your mental game.

Now, here's my call to action for you. Start implementing these techniques in your daily routine. Practice mindfulness, set SMART goals, and celebrate your small wins. Reflect on your experiences and learn from them. Build a support network that encourages you and holds you accountable. Embrace challenges as opportunities for growth, and always maintain a positive mindset. Remember, mental toughness isn't just for athletes; it's a life skill that can help you succeed in any area.

On a personal note, I want to express my gratitude for joining me on this journey. My passion for helping young athletes, parents, coaches and everyday people stems from my experiences and the belief that mental toughness can unlock your true potential. I've seen firsthand how these techniques can transform lives, and I hope they inspire you to reach new heights.

I leave you with this final thought:

> *"The only limit to our realization of tomorrow is our doubts of today."*
>
> — FRANKLIN D. ROOSEVELT

Believe in yourself, stay resilient, and keep pushing forward. Your journey to mental toughness and success is just beginning, and I can't wait to see all you achieve.

REFERENCES

Michael Jordan: Lessons in Greatness from the Flu Game ... https://www.linkedin.com/pulse/michael-jordan-lessons-greatness-from-flu-game-beyond-jayaraman-8yefe

Revisiting Growth Mindset as a Core Capacity of Sport ... https://applied-sportpsych.org/blog/2021/04/revisiting-growth-mindset-as-a-core-capacity-of-sport-psychology/

Angela Duckworth and the Research on 'Grit' https://americanradioworks.publicradio.org/features/tomorrows-college/grit/angela-duckworth-grit.html

The Influence of Emotional Intelligence on Performance in ...https://www.ncbi.nlm.nih.gov/pmc/articles/PMC6316207/

20 Mindfulness Exercises for Athletes https://purposesoulathletics.com/20-mindfulness-exercises-for-athletes/

How Michael Phelps Used Visualization to Stay Calm ... https://www.your-swimlog.com/michael-phelps-visualization/

*Science of Breath Work: Breathing for Athletes*https://blayze.io/blog/general/the-science-of-breathing-for-athletes

Rafael Nadal and His Various On-Court Rituals, Explained https://www.distractify.com/p/rafael-nadal-rituals

Sports Performance Anxiety: Causes, Signs, Tips to Cope https://www.healthline.com/health/sports-performance-anxiety

Cognitive-Behavioral Therapy (CBT) for Athletes https://behavioralhealth-centers.com/blog/athletes-anxiety-benefit-cognitive-behavioral-therapy/

The Unseen Consequences of Parental Pressure in Youth ... https://ilove-towatchyouplay.com/2023/08/22/the-unseen-consequences-of-parental-pressure-in-youth-sports/

Mental Health and Athletes https://www.athletesforhope.org/2019/05/mental-health-and-athletes/

Positive Daily Affirmations: Is There Science Behind It? https://positivepsychology.com/daily-affirmations/

Olympians Use Imagery as Mental Training https://www.nytimes.com/2014/02/23/sports/olympics/olympians-use-imagery-as-mental-training.html

Celebrating Small Wins: Nurturing Youth Athletes … https://isport360.com/celebrating-small-wins-nurturing-youth-athletes-confidence-and-joy/

The impact of athlete role models on youth development … https://moneysmartathlete.com/athlete-role-models/the-impact-of-athlete-role-models-on-youth-development-and-sports-participation/

Michael Jordan: A Story of Success, Determination, and … https://medium.com/@manlyzine.com/michael-jordan-a-story-of-success-determination-and-resilience-86f63b6ea389

Serena Williams Explains How Losses Have Made Her a … https://www.essentiallysports.com/wta-tennis-news-serena-williams-explains-how-losses-have-made-her-a-better-player/

Cyclist Lance Armstrong refuses to lose to cancer https://www.espn.com/espn/story/_/page/Mag15Racingthedemons/cyclist-lance-armstrong-refuses-lose-cancer-espn-magazine-archive

Bethany Hamilton: 20 Years After Shark Attack https://www.tiktok.com/@bethanyhamiltonofficial/video/7296295362690567466

*LeBron James Invests in His Mental Fitness and You Should…*https://mental-fitness.us/2020/02/lebron-james-invests-mental-fitness/

Tom Brady Workout: Tom's 9-Exercise High-Intensity Routine https://tb12sports.com/blogs/tb12/tom-brady-workout?srsltid=AfmBOoomQ-VfPGe2pSNsJ8usHJ2QbSgotYO6GEOTvDc0iflyzr798sSh

Mindfulness: the secret weapon of Michael Jordan and … https://www.marca.com/en/more-sports/2018/08/08/5b6b082f22601d291e8b45b9.html

Nutritional Considerations for Performance in Young Athletes https://www.ncbi.nlm.nih.gov/pmc/articles/PMC4590906/

Parents: Communicating with your child's coach https://www.osaa.org/docs/osaainfo/parentscommunicatingwithcoaches.pdf

Supporting Young Athletes: The Importance of Positive … https://medium.com/@thelittlefoxesclub/supporting-young-athletes-the-importance-of-positive-reinforcement-in-youth-sports-f727881cf19d

Setting Realistic Expectations for Youth Athletes https://www.momsteam.com/successful-parenting/setting-realistic-expectations-for-youth-athletes

Preventing Burnout in Youth Sports: Strategies for Success https://www.jerseywatch.com/blog/burnout-in-youth-sports

Why Learning is Important for Athletes - iSportz https://isportz.co/sports/why-learning-is-important-for-athletes

Motivating Young Athletes https://appliedsportpsych.org/resources/resources-for-coaches/motivating-young-athletes/

Emerging athletes' career transitions in professional sport https://www.ncbi.nlm.nih.gov/pmc/articles/PMC11254707/

Self-Reflection: Benefits and How to Practice https://www.verywellmind.com/self-reflection-importance-benefits-and-strategies-7500858